MALWARE REVERSE ENGINEERING

CRACKING THE CODE

4 BOOKS IN 1

BOOK 1
MALWARE REVERSE ENGINEERING ESSENTIALS: A BEGINNER'S GUIDE

BOOK 2
MASTERING MALWARE REVERSE ENGINEERING: FROM NOVICE TO EXPERT

BOOK 3
MALWARE ANALYSIS AND REVERSE ENGINEERING: A COMPREHENSIVE JOURNEY

BOOK 4
ADVANCED TECHNIQUES IN MALWARE REVERSE ENGINEERING: EXPERT-LEVEL INSIGHTS

ROB BOTWRIGHT

Published by Rob Botwright
Library of Congress Cataloging-in-Publication Data
ISBN 978-1-83938-602-2
Cover design by Rizzo

BOOK 1 - MALWARE REVERSE ENGINEERING ESSENTIALS: A BEGINNER'S GUIDE

BOOK 2 - MASTERING MALWARE REVERSE ENGINEERING: FROM NOVICE TO EXPERT

BOOK 3 - MALWARE ANALYSIS AND REVERSE ENGINEERING: A COMPREHENSIVE JOURNEY

BOOK 4 - ADVANCED TECHNIQUES IN MALWARE REVERSE ENGINEERING: EXPERT-LEVEL INSIGHTS

Introduction

In the intricate labyrinth of cyberspace, the presence of malevolent software, known as malware, looms as a persistent threat. Malware's ability to infiltrate, disrupt, and compromise digital systems knows no bounds. In this digital age, where every facet of our lives relies on technology, understanding and combating this perilous foe has become paramount. Welcome to "Malware Reverse Engineering: Cracking the Code" — a comprehensive journey through the realms of malware analysis and reverse engineering.

This book bundle embarks on a transformative voyage, spanning four meticulously crafted volumes, each tailored to a specific tier of expertise. Together, these volumes constitute a roadmap for anyone intrigued by the intricacies of malware and determined to become a proficient malware analyst, from novices taking their first steps to seasoned experts honing their skills.

Our journey begins with "Malware Reverse Engineering Essentials: A Beginner's Guide." Here, we lay the foundation for your understanding, introducing you to the world of malware and the fundamental concepts of reverse engineering. Even if you are a complete novice in this field, fear not; this volume is your gentle guide to grasping the basics.

Moving forward, "Mastering Malware Reverse Engineering: From Novice to Expert" becomes your bridge to deeper insights. Here, we delve into the intricate workings of malware and equip you with the skills to dissect and analyze a variety of malicious specimens. No longer a novice, you emerge from this volume as a capable analyst, eager to explore further.

"Malware Analysis and Reverse Engineering: A Comprehensive Journey" is where the journey reaches its zenith. In this book, we explore both static and dynamic analysis techniques, ensuring you are equipped with the holistic approach necessary to tackle malware comprehensively. The knowledge gained here forms the core of a proficient malware analyst's arsenal.

Our final volume, "Advanced Techniques in Malware Reverse Engineering: Expert-Level Insights," is the culmination of our journey. It unveils the most intricate and elusive aspects of malware analysis, from unraveling code obfuscation to dissecting complex communication protocols. Expert-level guidance and real-world case studies ensure you are prepared for the most challenging tasks in the field.

The battle against malware is relentless, and adversaries continually adapt their tactics. However, with the knowledge and skills acquired through these four volumes, you stand as a stalwart defender of digital systems. "Malware Reverse Engineering: Cracking the Code" is your compendium for the ongoing battle against cyber threats.

As we begin this journey together, we invite you to immerse yourself in the world of malware reverse engineering. Whether you are an enthusiast seeking knowledge, an aspiring analyst, or a seasoned expert, this book bundle promises to be your trusted companion. Join us as we uncover the secrets of malware, unravel their code, and safeguard the digital realm from their insidious presence.

BOOK 1
MALWARE REVERSE ENGINEERING ESSENTIALS
A BEGINNER'S GUIDE

ROB BOTWRIGHT

Chapter 1: Introduction to Malware and Reverse Engineering

The evolution of malware has been a relentless and ongoing battle between attackers and defenders in the digital realm. It's a story that spans decades, from the early days of simple viruses to the sophisticated and highly targeted threats we face today. Malware, short for "malicious software," encompasses a wide range of software programs designed with malicious intent, including viruses, worms, Trojans, ransomware, and spyware.

In the early days of computing, malware was relatively benign, often created as a form of digital vandalism or as experiments by curious programmers. The term "virus" was coined in the 1980s to describe self-replicating programs that could infect other programs and systems. These early viruses were primarily proof-of-concept creations, often spreading through floppy disks or shared files on early computer networks.

As the internet gained popularity in the late 1990s and early 2000s, malware authors began to see new opportunities for their creations. Worms like the infamous "ILOVEYOU" worm in 2000 exploited vulnerabilities in email systems and spread rapidly, causing widespread disruption and financial damage. This marked a shift from relatively harmless pranks to more malicious intent.

The early 2000s also saw the emergence of Trojans, which were malware disguised as legitimate software to trick users into running them. These Trojans could steal sensitive information, such as login credentials and financial data, and opened up new avenues for cybercriminals to profit from their malicious activities.

One of the most significant milestones in malware evolution was the rise of ransomware in the mid-2000s. Ransomware encrypts a victim's files and demands a ransom in exchange for the decryption key. This introduced a lucrative revenue stream for cybercriminals, as victims often felt compelled to pay to regain access to their data.

Malware authors continually adapted to security measures, employing techniques to evade detection and analysis. Rootkits, for example, became a staple in the malware toolkit. These stealthy pieces of software could hide their presence within a compromised system, making them difficult to detect.

In the past decade, targeted attacks have become increasingly prevalent, with advanced persistent threats (APTs) being a prime example. APTs are sophisticated and well-funded campaigns often sponsored by nation-states or criminal organizations. They employ a combination of advanced malware, social engineering, and zero-day vulnerabilities to breach high-value targets, such as government agencies and corporations.

The mobile revolution also brought with it a new frontier for malware. Malicious apps on smartphones and tablets could compromise personal data, spy on users, or even turn devices into bots for large-scale attacks. Mobile malware has become a growing concern in recent years.

To counter these evolving threats, the field of cybersecurity has also advanced significantly. Security companies and researchers continually develop new technologies and techniques to detect and mitigate malware. Signature-based antivirus software has given way to more sophisticated approaches, including behavior-based analysis and machine learning algorithms that can identify previously unknown threats.

Government agencies and international organizations have also joined the fight against malware. Cybersecurity laws and regulations have been enacted to hold cybercriminals accountable and promote cybersecurity best practices. International cooperation has become crucial in tracking down and apprehending cybercriminals operating across borders.

The battle against malware is ongoing, and it's a battle that will likely never end. As long as there is valuable data to exploit and financial gain to be had, cybercriminals will continue to adapt and evolve their tactics. Organizations and individuals must remain vigilant, keep their software up-to-date, practice good cybersecurity hygiene, and stay informed about emerging threats to protect themselves in this ever-changing digital landscape.

The role of reverse engineering in cybersecurity is pivotal, serving as a crucial tool in understanding and defending against malicious software and cyber threats. This practice involves dissecting and analyzing software or hardware to discern its underlying structure, functionality, and potential vulnerabilities. Reverse engineering empowers cybersecurity professionals to decipher the inner workings of malware, exploits, and other cyber threats. By unraveling these digital enigmas, experts can develop effective countermeasures and fortify defenses against future attacks.

At its core, reverse engineering acts as a digital detective, shedding light on the intentions and methods of cybercriminals. When a new malware strain emerges, reverse engineers delve into its code, identifying malicious functionalities, communication channels, and evasion techniques. This knowledge is invaluable for crafting precise detection signatures and devising strategies to thwart the threat's operations.

In the realm of vulnerability assessment, reverse engineering plays a fundamental role in uncovering weaknesses in software and hardware systems. Security researchers reverse engineer software applications and firmware to pinpoint vulnerabilities that could potentially be exploited by attackers. Identifying and patching these vulnerabilities is essential for preventing breaches and data compromises.

Moreover, reverse engineering extends its influence to the realm of digital forensics. When a security incident occurs, digital forensics experts utilize reverse engineering to scrutinize compromised systems, retrieve evidence, and reconstruct cybercrime scenarios. Reverse engineers help answer critical questions, such as how an attacker gained access, what actions were taken, and what data was compromised.

Reverse engineering is also instrumental in the analysis of network protocols. Cybersecurity professionals employ this practice to decipher communication protocols used by malware to exfiltrate data or receive commands from a remote server. Understanding these protocols allows defenders to detect and block malicious traffic effectively.

The impact of reverse engineering extends to hardware as well. In the domain of hardware security, reverse engineers assess the security of integrated circuits, microcontrollers, and other electronic components. They uncover potential weaknesses in hardware security mechanisms and devise strategies to protect against tampering and exploitation.

In essence, reverse engineering serves as a bridge between cybersecurity offense and defense. While some cybercriminals leverage reverse engineering to create and refine malicious tools, defenders harness the same techniques to dissect and neutralize these threats. This continuous cycle of analysis and adaptation propels the cybersecurity industry forward, enabling it to stay one step ahead of evolving cyber threats.

Reverse engineers employ a variety of tools and methodologies in their work. They use disassemblers to convert binary code into a human-readable form, revealing the logic and algorithms behind software applications. Debuggers allow them to step through code execution, inspect memory contents, and identify vulnerabilities. Decompilers assist in translating compiled code back into a higher-level programming language, aiding in the understanding of complex software.

Automated analysis tools, such as sandboxes and static analysis scanners, complement the efforts of reverse engineers. These tools provide rapid assessments of suspicious files and help prioritize items for manual examination. Machine learning and artificial intelligence are also making inroads into the field, offering the potential to automate certain aspects of reverse engineering and malware analysis.

One of the primary objectives of reverse engineering is to construct a detailed model of the software or hardware being analyzed. This model encompasses the program's control flow, data flow, and logic structures. Reverse engineers painstakingly document their findings, creating diagrams, flowcharts, and reports that serve as essential references for security professionals and developers alike.

In the context of cybersecurity, reverse engineering facilitates the development of robust security solutions. By gaining insights into the tactics and techniques employed by cyber adversaries, security teams can devise strategies to mitigate risks effectively. Reverse engineering aids in the creation of intrusion detection systems, firewalls, and antivirus software that can identify and block malicious activity.

Moreover, reverse engineering supports incident response efforts. When a security breach occurs, organizations rely on the expertise of reverse engineers to analyze the compromised systems, identify the attack vector, and determine the extent of the damage. This information is vital for containing the incident, recovering data, and fortifying defenses against future attacks.

The field of reverse engineering is not confined solely to responding to threats; it also plays a proactive role in threat intelligence. Security researchers actively engage in reverse engineering to uncover emerging threats and vulnerabilities. By analyzing malware and exploit techniques, they provide early warnings to the cybersecurity community, enabling organizations to fortify their defenses before cybercriminals can exploit weaknesses.

Reverse engineering is a multifaceted discipline that encompasses a wide range of skills and knowledge. Professionals in this field must possess a deep understanding of programming languages, operating systems, network protocols, and hardware architectures. They must also stay abreast of emerging technologies and cyber threats, as the landscape continually evolves.

The legal and ethical aspects of reverse engineering are also critical considerations. In many cases, reverse engineering is conducted within the boundaries of applicable laws and industry standards. However, there are legal and ethical gray areas, particularly when analyzing proprietary software or hardware. Researchers must navigate these challenges while ensuring their actions are within legal constraints.

In summary, the role of reverse engineering in cybersecurity cannot be overstated. It serves as a linchpin in the ongoing battle against cyber threats, enabling defenders to understand, detect, and mitigate malicious activities effectively. With the relentless evolution of cyber threats, reverse engineering remains an indispensable practice that empowers cybersecurity professionals to stay vigilant and proactive in safeguarding digital landscapes.

Chapter 2: Setting Up Your Malware Analysis Environment

Selecting the right tools for any task is paramount, but in the realm of cybersecurity and reverse engineering, it takes on a heightened level of significance. The choice of tools can significantly impact the efficiency and effectiveness of your efforts. The world of cybersecurity offers a vast array of software, hardware, and techniques, each designed to serve specific purposes. The challenge lies in identifying the tools that align with your objectives, whether you're analyzing malware, assessing vulnerabilities, or conducting digital forensics.

One of the fundamental considerations when choosing tools is the nature of the task at hand. For instance, if you are analyzing a suspected malware sample, you will require a different set of tools compared to assessing the security of a network or conducting forensic analysis on a compromised system. Understanding the specific requirements of your project is essential to making informed tool selections.

The expertise and experience of the personnel involved also play a crucial role in tool selection. Skilled professionals may opt for more advanced and specialized tools, while beginners may prefer user-friendly options with extensive documentation and community support. The availability of training resources and the learning curve associated with a tool should factor into your decision-making process.

Compatibility with your existing environment is another key consideration. The tools you choose should integrate seamlessly with your current systems and processes. Compatibility issues can lead to inefficiencies and disruptions in your workflow, potentially impacting the quality of your analysis or the timeliness of your response to security incidents.

Open-source tools, which are developed and maintained by a community of volunteers, offer numerous advantages. They are often free to use, which can be especially appealing for organizations with limited budgets. Open-source tools also tend to be transparent, allowing users to review the source code and verify their security. Moreover, the open-source community often provides extensive support and updates, ensuring that the tools remain relevant and reliable.

However, commercial tools have their merits as well. They are typically backed by dedicated companies that offer professional support, training, and regular updates. Commercial tools may have more polished user interfaces and additional features tailored to specific use cases. When evaluating commercial tools, consider factors such as licensing costs, support options, and the track record of the vendor.

The choice between command-line and graphical user interface (GUI) tools is another decision point. Command-line tools, while often more powerful and flexible, require a higher level of technical expertise. GUI tools, on the other hand, offer a more user-friendly experience but may lack certain advanced capabilities. The choice between these two interfaces depends on your proficiency and the specific tasks you need to accomplish.

Tool compatibility and interoperability are crucial considerations, especially when working on complex projects or within large organizations. Tools should seamlessly share data and results with one another, allowing for a streamlined workflow. Compatibility issues can lead to data loss, redundancy, and inefficiencies.

Another important aspect to consider is the reputation and trustworthiness of the tools you select. This is particularly relevant when dealing with security-related tasks. Reputable tools have been vetted by the cybersecurity community and are less likely to contain vulnerabilities or backdoors that could be exploited by malicious actors.

The availability of documentation and community support is invaluable, especially when working with complex or less-known tools. A vibrant user community can provide assistance, troubleshooting tips, and best practices to help you make the most of your chosen tools.

Updates and maintenance should not be overlooked. Cyber threats evolve rapidly, and tools must keep pace to remain effective. Regular updates and patches ensure that your tools are equipped to handle the latest challenges and vulnerabilities.

Scalability is an essential factor for organizations with growing or changing needs. Ensure that the tools you select can scale with your requirements, whether that involves handling larger datasets, accommodating more users, or expanding your analysis capabilities.

Security considerations are paramount in the selection process. Malicious actors may target cybersecurity tools, so it's crucial to choose tools that are themselves secure. Regularly updating and patching your tools is essential to mitigate security risks. Additionally, consider tools that offer encryption and authentication features to protect sensitive data.

Lastly, budget constraints are a reality for many organizations. While open-source tools can be cost-effective, the total cost of ownership should be evaluated. This includes factors like training, support, and ongoing maintenance. Commercial tools may have upfront costs, but they may also offer a comprehensive package that can ultimately reduce operational costs.

In summary, choosing the right tools in cybersecurity and reverse engineering is a decision that can greatly influence the outcome of your projects and the security of your systems. It requires a careful assessment of your specific needs, your team's expertise, and the compatibility, trustworthiness, and scalability of the tools under consideration. By making informed choices, you can ensure that your cybersecurity efforts are both effective and efficient.

Configuring a secure analysis environment is a foundational step in the practice of malware reverse engineering and cybersecurity research. It serves as the protective fortress where you examine and dissect potentially dangerous software and files. This environment is designed to shield your host system and network from the inherent risks associated with handling malicious code. In essence, it creates a controlled and isolated space where you can safely conduct your analysis without exposing your primary infrastructure to harm.

The primary goal of configuring a secure analysis environment is to contain any potential threats and minimize the chances of unintended consequences. One fundamental principle is to create a clear separation between the analysis environment and your everyday computing environment. This isolation ensures that malware or malicious files cannot easily escape and propagate through your network or infect your primary system.

The first step in configuring a secure analysis environment is to establish a dedicated and isolated physical or virtual machine. This machine should be separate from your daily-use computer to prevent any cross-contamination. You can create a virtual machine using hypervisor software such as VMware, VirtualBox, or Hyper-V. Virtualization offers the advantage of flexibility, allowing you to snapshot and clone analysis environments for different purposes.

Once you have your isolated environment, it's crucial to ensure that the host system is fully patched and updated. This includes the operating system, hypervisor, and any software components used in the analysis environment. Unpatched vulnerabilities on the host system could potentially be exploited by malware attempting to escape the analysis environment.

An important aspect of configuring a secure analysis environment is network isolation. Ideally, the analysis environment should be disconnected from the internet and any sensitive internal networks. This minimizes the risk of malware communicating with command and control servers or spreading to other systems on your network. You can achieve network isolation by configuring the virtual machine's network settings or by using a physically separate network.

Another critical element is the use of network-level security controls, such as firewalls and intrusion detection systems. These controls can be implemented within the analysis environment to monitor and filter network traffic. In the event that malware attempts to establish network connections, these security measures can help detect and block suspicious activities.

To further enhance security, consider implementing network segmentation within your analysis environment. This involves creating multiple virtual subnets to separate different stages of the analysis process. For example, you might have a dedicated subnet for capturing network traffic and another for executing potentially malicious code. This segmentation adds an extra layer of protection by limiting the scope of any potential breaches.

Maintaining the integrity of the analysis environment is paramount. Regularly take snapshots or backups of the clean state of the environment. These snapshots serve as restore points that you can return to if the environment becomes compromised during analysis. It's essential to document and label these snapshots to ensure you can easily identify and revert to a trusted state.

Another security measure is the use of access controls and permissions within the analysis environment. Limit user privileges to only those necessary for conducting the analysis. This principle of least privilege reduces the potential impact of security breaches and minimizes the damage that malware can inflict within the environment.

In addition to network isolation, consider creating a dedicated storage environment for handling potentially malicious files. Isolate storage resources, such as network-attached storage (NAS) or external drives, to prevent malware from spreading to your primary storage systems. Use encryption and access controls to secure the dedicated storage and ensure that it is only accessible within the analysis environment.

Sandboxing is a valuable technique for safely executing and analyzing suspicious code within the analysis environment. Sandboxes are controlled environments that restrict the actions of executed programs. They can prevent malware from making system-wide changes or accessing sensitive data on the host system. Sandboxing tools are available for various operating systems and can be customized to meet your specific analysis requirements.

One key consideration in configuring a secure analysis environment is the selection of the analysis tools themselves. Ensure that the tools you choose are reputable and well-maintained. Vulnerabilities in analysis tools can pose a risk to the security of your environment, so regularly update and patch them.

Implementing robust endpoint security measures within the analysis environment is also crucial. This includes antivirus software, intrusion detection systems, and host-based firewalls. While the primary goal is to analyze malware, there is always a risk of accidental execution or the presence of secondary threats. Endpoint security controls can help mitigate these risks.

Furthermore, consider using virtualization-based security solutions that leverage hardware-assisted isolation technologies, such as Intel VT-x and AMD-V. These technologies provide an additional layer of protection by isolating the analysis environment at the hardware level. This can be particularly effective in preventing malware from escaping the virtual machine.

In summary, configuring a secure analysis environment is a foundational step in the practice of malware reverse engineering and cybersecurity research. It involves creating a controlled and isolated space where you can safely analyze potentially malicious code without exposing your primary infrastructure to harm. By following best practices, such as network isolation, access controls, and regular updates, you can minimize risks and conduct effective and secure analysis.

Chapter 3: Fundamentals of Assembly Language

Assembly language is a low-level programming language that serves as a bridge between machine code and high-level programming languages. It provides a human-readable representation of a computer's binary instructions, allowing programmers to write code that directly interacts with a computer's central processing unit (CPU). While high-level languages like C++, Java, and Python are more accessible and user-friendly, assembly language is the closest one can get to the computer's hardware without dealing with raw binary code.

In assembly language, each instruction corresponds to a single machine instruction or operation that the CPU can execute. This means that assembly programs are specific to the computer's architecture, as different CPUs have different instruction sets. Assembly language is machine-dependent, and programmers must be familiar with the architecture of the target CPU to write effective assembly code.

One of the defining characteristics of assembly language is its use of mnemonic codes to represent machine instructions. These mnemonic codes are more human-readable than binary code but still map directly to the CPU's binary instructions. For example, instead of writing the binary code "0010101101100010" to add two numbers, an assembly programmer might use the mnemonic "ADD" followed by the names of the registers or memory locations to be added.

Assembly language also allows programmers to work with registers, which are small, high-speed storage locations within the CPU. Registers are used to hold data temporarily during computations and are an essential part of assembly programming. Programmers must manage the allocation and usage of registers carefully to optimize code and avoid overwriting important data.

In addition to registers, assembly language provides access to memory locations. Programmers can load data from memory into registers, perform operations on that data, and store the results back in memory. Managing memory is a critical aspect of assembly programming, as improper memory access can lead to bugs and security vulnerabilities.

Assembly language programs are typically written in a text editor or an integrated development environment (IDE) specifically designed for assembly programming. Programmers write code using the mnemonic instructions and symbols that represent memory addresses or labels within the program. These symbols help make the code more readable and maintainable.

The assembly code is then assembled or compiled into machine code using an assembler. The assembler translates the mnemonic instructions and symbols into the binary instructions that the CPU can execute directly. The resulting machine code can be executed on the target computer, where it performs the specified operations.

Understanding assembly language is valuable for several reasons. First, it provides insight into the inner workings of a computer's CPU and memory management. Programmers who are proficient in assembly language can write code that is highly optimized and efficient, as they have a deep understanding of how the hardware operates.

Second, assembly language is sometimes necessary for tasks that require low-level system access, such as writing device drivers, operating system kernels, or embedded systems code. In these cases, higher-level languages may not provide the level of control needed to interact with hardware directly.

Third, reverse engineering and malware analysis often involve examining binary code, which may require knowledge of assembly language. Analysts use assembly language to disassemble and understand the functionality of binary executables, helping them identify security vulnerabilities or analyze malicious software.

Fourth, assembly language is a valuable skill for cybersecurity professionals, as it allows them to understand and exploit vulnerabilities in software and systems. Ethical hackers and security researchers use assembly language to identify and patch vulnerabilities, protect systems, and develop security tools.

Fifth, learning assembly language can be intellectually rewarding. It challenges programmers to think at a low level, where they must understand the intricacies of CPU architecture, memory management, and data representation. This deep understanding of computing fundamentals can enhance problem-solving skills and contribute to a broader understanding of computer science.

One of the challenges of learning assembly language is that it can initially appear complex and cryptic, especially to those accustomed to higher-level programming languages. Assembly code is often dense, and each instruction must be carefully crafted to perform a specific task. Additionally, debugging assembly code can be more challenging than debugging code written in higher-level languages, as there are no built-in abstractions or error-checking mechanisms.

To become proficient in assembly language, programmers must invest time in learning the specific instruction set and architecture of the target CPU. They should also practice writing assembly code for various tasks, from simple arithmetic operations to more complex algorithms. Gaining experience and developing problem-solving skills are essential for mastering assembly programming.

Fortunately, there are numerous resources available to help individuals learn assembly language. Textbooks, online tutorials, and educational websites offer comprehensive guides and examples. Additionally, many universities and educational institutions offer courses that cover assembly language programming as part of their computer science and computer engineering curricula.

In summary, assembly language is a low-level programming language that provides a direct interface to a computer's CPU and memory. It allows programmers to write code using mnemonic instructions and symbols that represent machine instructions and memory addresses. Assembly language is valuable for understanding computer architecture, writing low-level system code, analyzing binary executables, and enhancing cybersecurity skills. Learning assembly language may be challenging, but it offers a deeper understanding of computing fundamentals and the ability to work closely with hardware. Basic assembly language instructions serve as the foundational building blocks for writing programs in assembly language. These instructions are the elemental operations that a computer's central processing unit (CPU) can execute directly. Understanding and mastering these instructions is essential for programming in assembly language and gaining insights into how a computer's hardware functions.

At the core of assembly language are instructions that manipulate data, perform arithmetic and logic operations, and control program flow. One of the most fundamental instructions is the "MOV" instruction, short for "move," which transfers data from one location to another. The "MOV" instruction can move data between registers, memory locations, and immediate values.

Arithmetic operations are a fundamental part of any programming language, and assembly language is no exception. Assembly instructions like "ADD," "SUB," "MUL" (multiply), and "DIV" (divide) allow programmers to perform basic arithmetic operations on data. These instructions are used extensively in numerical computations and data manipulation.

Logical operations, such as "AND," "OR," and "XOR," enable programmers to manipulate and compare bits within data. These operations are essential for tasks like bitwise manipulation, flag setting, and data masking.

Conditional branching instructions are used to control program flow based on specific conditions. The "JMP" (jump) instruction allows programmers to unconditionally transfer control to another part of the program. Conditional branching instructions like "JZ" (jump if zero), "JNZ" (jump if not zero), "JE" (jump if equal), and "JNE" (jump if not equal) enable programmers to implement decision-making logic in their code.

Assembly language also provides instructions for comparing data, such as "CMP" (compare) and "TEST." These instructions are often used in conjunction with conditional branching instructions to implement conditional statements and loops.

Data manipulation instructions extend beyond simple arithmetic and logical operations. Assembly language includes instructions for shifting and rotating bits within data. "SHL" (shift left), "SHR" (shift right), "ROL" (rotate left), and "ROR" (rotate right) are examples of instructions that perform bit-level operations.

Loading and storing data in memory is a critical aspect of assembly programming. Instructions like "LOAD" and "STORE" are used to transfer data between registers and memory locations. Memory addressing modes, such as direct addressing, indirect addressing, and indexed addressing, provide flexibility in specifying the source and destination of data transfers.

Conditional execution instructions, such as "CALL" and "RET" (return), enable the implementation of subroutines and function calls. Subroutines allow programmers to modularize their code and reuse specific functionality, enhancing code organization and maintainability.

Assembly language also includes instructions for interrupt handling, enabling interaction with external devices and services. Interrupt instructions like "INT" (interrupt) are used to trigger specific routines or services provided by the operating system or hardware.

Programmers must become familiar with the registers available on the target CPU, as registers are essential for temporary data storage and manipulation. Common registers include the accumulator (often denoted as "AX"), general-purpose registers (e.g., "BX," "CX," "DX"), and index registers (e.g., "SI" and "DI"). Understanding the purpose and limitations of each register is crucial for effective assembly programming.

Condition flags play a significant role in assembly language programming. Flags are bits within the CPU's status register that indicate the outcome of arithmetic and logical operations. Flags like the zero flag, carry flag, and overflow flag provide information about the result of an operation and are used in conditional branching instructions to make decisions.

Assembly language instructions are typically written using a mnemonic followed by operands, registers, and memory addresses. For example, the "MOV" instruction might appear as "MOV AX, BX," indicating that the contents of register BX are moved to register AX. Operand order and syntax may vary depending on the specific assembly language and CPU architecture.

Learning assembly language instructions requires practice and hands-on experience. Programmers often write simple programs to experiment with different instructions and observe their effects on data and program flow. Assembler tools are used to convert human-readable assembly code into machine code that can be executed on the target CPU.

While assembly language instructions provide a level of control and optimization not achievable in higher-level programming languages, they come with challenges. Assembly programming can be time-consuming and error-prone, as programmers must manage low-level details, such as memory allocation and register usage, manually. Additionally, debugging assembly code can be more challenging, as there are no high-level abstractions to simplify the process.

However, assembly language remains a valuable skill for specific tasks, such as writing low-level system code, optimizing performance-critical code, and conducting reverse engineering and malware analysis. Proficiency in assembly language can provide a deeper understanding of computer architecture and hardware, making it a valuable asset for computer scientists, security experts, and embedded systems developers.

In summary, basic assembly language instructions are the fundamental operations that a computer's CPU can execute directly. These instructions encompass data manipulation, arithmetic and logic operations, conditional branching, and program control. Understanding assembly language instructions is essential for writing low-level code, optimizing performance, and gaining insights into computer hardware. While assembly programming can be challenging, it offers a level of control and efficiency that is valuable for specific applications in the field of computer science.

Chapter 4: Dissecting Malware Samples

Understanding the anatomy of malware is a crucial aspect of cybersecurity and malware analysis, as it allows security professionals to dissect and comprehend the inner workings of malicious software. Malware, short for malicious software, is a broad term that encompasses a wide range of malicious code designed with harmful intent. This code can include viruses, worms, Trojans, ransomware, spyware, and more, each with its unique characteristics and functionalities.

Breaking down the anatomy of malware involves examining the various components and behaviors that make up a malicious program. At its core, malware consists of a payload and a delivery mechanism. The payload is the malicious code that performs harmful actions, while the delivery mechanism is the means by which the malware is introduced to a target system.

The payload of malware typically includes a set of instructions that carry out specific actions, such as stealing data, compromising system integrity, or providing unauthorized access to a system. These instructions are often concealed within the malware's code, making them difficult to detect without thorough analysis.

Malware payloads can range from relatively simple to highly sophisticated. Some malware may perform basic tasks, such as displaying unwanted advertisements or redirecting web traffic. Others may be designed to execute complex attacks, such as exploiting software vulnerabilities to gain control over a system or network.

The delivery mechanism of malware determines how it is distributed and executed on a target system. Malware can be introduced through various means, including email attachments, malicious websites, infected software downloads, and removable media like USB drives. Social engineering tactics, such as phishing emails and deceptive website content, are often used to trick users into triggering the delivery mechanism.

Once introduced to a target system, malware typically goes through several stages of execution. The first stage often involves gaining a foothold on the system by exploiting vulnerabilities or using social engineering techniques to deceive the user or system administrator. Once the malware is executed, it may attempt to establish persistence on the system to ensure it can survive reboots and system changes.

Persistence mechanisms can include modifying system settings, creating hidden files or directories, and adding registry entries. These tactics ensure that the malware remains active and continues to execute its malicious code even after initial infection.

Malware may also employ techniques to evade detection and analysis. These techniques can include using encryption or obfuscation to hide its code, altering its behavior in response to security tools, or employing anti-analysis measures to thwart reverse engineering attempts.

One critical aspect of malware anatomy is its ability to communicate with external entities, often referred to as command and control (C2) servers or botnet controllers. Malware can establish network connections to these external entities, allowing attackers to remotely control the infected system, transmit stolen data, or receive commands to carry out further malicious actions.

The communication between malware and C2 servers is typically hidden within network traffic, making it challenging to detect. Security analysts must closely monitor network traffic and analyze patterns to identify potential C2 communications and take appropriate action to block or investigate them.

Another essential component of malware anatomy is its ability to propagate or spread to other systems. Some malware, such as worms, are explicitly designed to self-replicate and spread to other vulnerable systems without requiring user interaction. Worms can exploit vulnerabilities in network services or software to propagate rapidly.

Other malware relies on user interaction or social engineering tactics to spread. For example, email attachments containing malware may be distributed to a wide audience, with the hope that recipients will open the attachments, triggering the malware's execution.

Understanding the behavior and capabilities of malware is essential for effective detection, analysis, and mitigation. Security professionals use a variety of tools and techniques to analyze malware samples and identify their characteristics. These tools may include antivirus scanners, sandbox environments, and specialized malware analysis platforms.

Static analysis involves examining the malware's code without executing it. Analysts inspect the code to identify known patterns or signatures associated with malicious behavior. Dynamic analysis, on the other hand, involves running the malware in a controlled environment, such as a sandbox, to observe its behavior and interactions with the system.

Behavioral analysis focuses on understanding how the malware interacts with the host system, including the files it accesses, system calls it makes, and network traffic it generates. This approach can provide insights into the malware's intent and functionality.

Signature-based detection relies on predefined patterns or signatures of known malware to identify malicious files or activities. Heuristic and behavior-based detection techniques, on the other hand, look for patterns of behavior that are indicative of malicious intent, even if the specific malware is previously unknown.

In addition to traditional detection methods, machine learning and artificial intelligence are increasingly used to analyze and detect malware. These advanced techniques can identify subtle and previously unseen patterns of malicious behavior, enhancing the ability to detect evolving threats.

Malware analysis is a multidisciplinary field that requires a deep understanding of computer science, networking, programming, and cybersecurity. It also demands constant vigilance and adaptation, as malware authors continually evolve their tactics and techniques to evade detection and analysis.

In summary, breaking down the anatomy of malware is a critical task for cybersecurity professionals and analysts. It involves understanding the components, behaviors, and delivery mechanisms that make up malicious software. By dissecting and comprehending malware, security experts can develop effective strategies to detect, analyze, and mitigate threats, helping to protect systems and data from harm.

Tools for dissecting malware samples are indispensable in the field of cybersecurity and malware analysis, as they provide the means to examine and understand the inner workings of malicious software. These tools encompass a wide range of software applications and utilities designed to aid security professionals in analyzing and dissecting malware for the purpose of threat detection, reverse engineering, and developing mitigation strategies.

One of the fundamental categories of tools for malware sample dissection includes static analysis tools. Static analysis tools allow analysts to examine the code and structure of a malware sample without executing it. These tools can reveal valuable information about the sample's file format, embedded resources, and code logic.

Disassemblers are a type of static analysis tool that translates executable code into a human-readable assembly language representation. This enables analysts to study the low-level instructions and logic flow of the malware. Popular disassemblers include IDA Pro, Ghidra, and radare2, which provide extensive disassembly capabilities and support for various executable file formats.

Another category of static analysis tools is decompilers, which convert compiled code back into a higher-level programming language. Decompilers are particularly useful when analyzing complex malware written in languages like C or C++. They help analysts understand the functionality of the malware by presenting code in a more familiar format. Ghidra and Hex-Rays IDA Pro both offer decompilation features.

Static analysis tools also include file analysis utilities that examine the structure and content of a malware sample's file, such as header information, resource data, and embedded files. Tools like PE Explorer and Resource Hacker are commonly used for inspecting the attributes and resources of Windows executable files.

Dynamic analysis tools are another crucial category for dissecting malware samples. Unlike static analysis, dynamic analysis involves running the malware in a controlled environment to observe its behavior. This approach is valuable for understanding how the malware interacts with the host system, its network activity, and its payload execution.

Sandbox environments are a fundamental component of dynamic analysis tools. Sandboxes provide a controlled and isolated environment where malware samples can be executed without affecting the host system. Popular sandbox solutions like Cuckoo Sandbox and VMRay Analyzer offer automated analysis and behavior monitoring capabilities, making them valuable tools for dissecting malware.

Network analysis tools are essential for monitoring and capturing network traffic generated by malware during dynamic analysis. Tools like Wireshark and tcpdump allow analysts to inspect network packets, identify communication with command and control servers, and determine the scope of the malware's network activity.

Dynamic analysis tools also encompass debugging and monitoring utilities that help analysts track the execution flow of malware samples and inspect their runtime behavior. Debuggers like OllyDbg and WinDbg are commonly used for this purpose, allowing analysts to set breakpoints, examine registers, and inspect memory during execution.

Memory analysis tools play a vital role in dissecting malware that manipulates or injects code into the memory of a compromised system. These tools enable analysts to inspect the contents of system memory, identify malicious processes, and uncover the presence of rootkits or other memory-resident malware. Volatility and Rekall are popular open-source memory analysis frameworks frequently used by analysts.

Behavioral analysis tools are designed to monitor the actions and interactions of malware with the host system and applications. These tools focus on identifying the behavioral patterns exhibited by malware samples during execution. Behavior-based analysis can detect malicious activities, such as file system modifications, registry changes, or privilege escalation attempts.

Signature-based detection tools are designed to recognize known malware patterns or signatures within files or network traffic. Antivirus and endpoint security solutions often employ signature-based detection to identify and quarantine malicious files or processes. These tools rely on regularly updated signature databases to stay current with emerging threats.

Intrusion detection and prevention systems (IDS/IPS) are network-based security tools that can also aid in the dissection of malware. They monitor network traffic and identify patterns or behaviors indicative of malicious activity. When configured to record detected threats, IDS/IPS logs can provide valuable insights for analyzing and dissecting malware-related network traffic.

Machine learning and artificial intelligence (AI) are increasingly integrated into malware analysis tools to enhance detection and dissection capabilities. These advanced techniques can identify complex and previously unknown malware patterns or behaviors by analyzing large datasets and learning from historical malware samples.

In summary, tools for dissecting malware samples are a critical resource for cybersecurity professionals and analysts tasked with understanding and mitigating threats. These tools encompass a wide range of capabilities, including static and dynamic analysis, behavioral analysis, signature-based detection, intrusion detection, and machine learning. By utilizing these tools effectively, analysts can uncover the inner workings of malware, identify its malicious behavior, and develop strategies to protect systems and networks from harm.

Chapter 5: Static Analysis Techniques

File analysis and metadata examination are essential components of digital forensics and cybersecurity, allowing investigators and analysts to gain valuable insights into the content, origin, and history of digital files. In today's digital age, files store a wealth of information, and understanding how to analyze them is crucial for uncovering evidence, identifying threats, and ensuring data integrity.

File analysis begins with the examination of file attributes, such as file size, creation date, modification date, and access date. These attributes can provide initial clues about a file's origin and usage, potentially revealing suspicious or anomalous behavior. For example, a file modified or accessed at unusual times may indicate unauthorized access or tampering.

Metadata, often referred to as "data about data," plays a significant role in file analysis. Metadata includes information embedded within files that describe their characteristics, history, and relationships. Common types of metadata include author information, document properties, timestamps, and version history.

Understanding the various types of metadata associated with different file formats is essential for extracting valuable information during file analysis. For example, in a Microsoft Word document, metadata may include the author's name, document title, word count, and the date of creation. This metadata can be examined to determine the document's source and usage history.

Metadata can also be embedded in image files, audio files, and email messages. Image files may contain information about the camera used to capture the image, the date it was taken, and even geographic coordinates. Audio files may include metadata such as artist, album, and track information. Email messages often carry a rich set of metadata, including sender and recipient details, timestamps, and email server information.

In addition to standard metadata, some file formats support the inclusion of custom or application-specific metadata. For instance, Adobe PDF documents can contain metadata related to annotations, bookmarks, and document properties. Video files may store metadata about codecs, frame rates, and video resolutions.

File analysis tools and techniques enable investigators to extract and examine metadata from digital files. Tools like ExifTool, FOCA, and Metadata Extractor are commonly used for extracting metadata from various file formats. These tools can help reveal hidden information and provide context for analyzing files in digital forensics investigations.

Examination of file content is another crucial aspect of file analysis. Beyond metadata, the actual content of files can contain valuable evidence or threats. Content analysis can involve the examination of text documents, spreadsheets, code, images, and multimedia files. It often requires specialized tools and techniques tailored to specific file formats.

Text analysis tools can be employed to search for keywords, phrases, or patterns within documents. This is particularly useful in e-discovery, where legal professionals search for relevant information in large volumes of text documents. Text analysis tools can also be used to identify sensitive data, such as personally identifiable information (PII) or intellectual property, within documents.

Multimedia analysis tools enable the examination of images, audio, and video files. Image analysis can involve the identification of objects, faces, or patterns within images.

For audio and video files, analysis tools can extract metadata related to codec information, timestamps, and frame rates. Additionally, speech recognition and sentiment analysis can be applied to audio content.

Code analysis tools are essential for examining executable files, scripts, and malware samples. These tools disassemble or decompile code to reveal its logic, functions, and potential vulnerabilities. In the case of malware analysis, code examination can help identify malicious behavior and reverse engineer the malware to understand its functionality.

File carving is a forensic technique used to recover and analyze files that have been deleted or partially overwritten. File carving tools scan storage media for file signatures and data structures, allowing investigators to reconstruct and examine files that may not be accessible through traditional file system navigation.

Steganography detection is a specialized area of file analysis that focuses on identifying hidden information within files. Steganography techniques involve embedding data within the pixels of images, the least significant bits of audio files, or other file types. Steganography detection tools can reveal the presence of hidden content and extract it for further examination.

File analysis and metadata examination are not limited to digital forensics; they also play a crucial role in cybersecurity. Threat intelligence analysts often analyze files to identify indicators of compromise (IOCs) and analyze the tactics, techniques, and procedures (TTPs) used by attackers. By examining file artifacts, security professionals can detect and respond to cyber threats effectively.

In cybersecurity, file analysis includes the examination of malicious files and potentially malicious files, such as those received in phishing emails or downloaded from suspicious websites. Sandboxing and detonation chambers are used to execute potentially malicious files in a controlled environment, allowing analysts to observe their behavior and determine their threat level.

File analysis tools in cybersecurity may also involve the use of threat intelligence feeds and reputation databases to assess the trustworthiness of files and URLs. These tools can help security teams make informed decisions about whether to block, quarantine, or allow the execution of files based on their reputation and known threats.

In summary, file analysis and metadata examination are indispensable skills and techniques in the fields of digital forensics and cybersecurity. Understanding how to analyze file attributes, extract metadata, and examine file content is crucial for uncovering evidence, identifying threats, and protecting digital assets. Whether investigating a digital crime or defending against cyber threats, professionals in these fields rely on file analysis to gain insights and make informed decisions. Strings analysis and pattern recognition are fundamental techniques in the fields of data analysis, text processing, and cybersecurity, enabling the identification of meaningful information within a sequence of characters or data. Strings, in this context, refer to sequences of alphanumeric characters, symbols, or binary data that can be analyzed for various purposes, such as extracting insights from text, detecting patterns in data, and identifying anomalies or threats.

Pattern recognition, as a broader concept, encompasses the ability to identify recurring structures or sequences within data, enabling the discovery of regularities and trends. It is a fundamental process in fields ranging from machine learning and natural language processing to signal processing and computer vision. In the context of strings analysis, pattern recognition is particularly valuable for identifying specific sequences or structures within textual or binary data.

One of the primary goals of strings analysis is to extract meaningful information from text or data that may appear disorganized or unstructured at first glance. Textual data can be found in various forms, including documents, emails, social media posts, and more. Strings analysis techniques aim to process and interpret this text to uncover insights, sentiments, or hidden patterns.

Strings analysis often begins with basic operations like searching for specific keywords or phrases within a body of text. This allows analysts to quickly identify relevant content or topics of interest. For example, searching for keywords like "cybersecurity" or "malware" within a collection of news articles can help researchers find articles related to these topics.

Regular expressions are powerful tools used in strings analysis for pattern matching and extraction. Regular expressions are patterns that define a set of strings with a specific structure or format. Analysts can use regular expressions to extract email addresses, phone numbers, dates, or other structured data from text. For example, a regular expression can be designed to recognize and extract all email addresses from a given document.

In addition to basic search and extraction, strings analysis techniques involve the use of natural language processing (NLP) and text analytics. NLP allows for the processing and understanding of human language, enabling tasks such as sentiment analysis, named entity recognition, and language translation. Sentiment analysis, for instance, helps determine the emotional tone of text, which can be valuable in assessing public opinion or customer sentiment.

Named entity recognition (NER) is a specific strings analysis task that involves identifying and categorizing entities within text, such as names of people, organizations, locations, and dates. NER is crucial in various applications, including information retrieval, document categorization, and data linking. Text classification is another strings analysis technique that involves categorizing text documents into predefined categories or topics. Machine learning algorithms are often employed to automatically classify documents based on their content. For instance, a machine learning model can classify news articles into categories like "politics," "sports," or "technology" based on the text content.

Strings analysis also plays a significant role in data mining and data preprocessing. In data mining, analysts use various techniques to discover patterns, associations, and correlations within large datasets. Frequent pattern mining, for example, helps identify recurring sequences or combinations of items in transactional data, which is valuable in market basket analysis and recommendation systems.

In cybersecurity, strings analysis is a critical component of threat detection and intrusion detection systems. Security analysts use strings analysis techniques to identify known indicators of compromise (IOCs) within network traffic, logs, and files. IOCs may include specific patterns or strings associated with malware, suspicious IP addresses, or unauthorized access attempts.

Advanced cybersecurity tools use machine learning and anomaly detection to recognize abnormal patterns or behaviors within network traffic or system logs. These tools can identify deviations from normal behavior, which may indicate a security breach or potential threat. For example, a cybersecurity system might detect unusual strings or patterns of network traffic that suggest a Distributed Denial of Service (DDoS) attack.

Pattern recognition is closely related to strings analysis, as it involves the identification of recurring structures or sequences within data, whether in text, images, audio, or other formats. Machine learning algorithms, particularly those based on deep learning, have advanced pattern recognition capabilities in various domains.

In computer vision, pattern recognition algorithms can identify objects, faces, or shapes within images and videos. These algorithms are used in applications such as facial recognition, object detection, and autonomous driving. Pattern recognition in audio processing enables tasks like speech recognition, music genre classification, and audio event detection.

In summary, strings analysis and pattern recognition are essential techniques for extracting meaningful information, identifying patterns, and recognizing regularities within textual, binary, or structured data. These techniques are employed in various domains, from data analysis and natural language processing to cybersecurity and computer vision. Whether it's extracting insights from text, detecting anomalies in network traffic, or recognizing objects in images, strings analysis and pattern recognition are indispensable tools for data analysis and information discovery.

Chapter 6: Dynamic Analysis and Debugging

Setting up dynamic analysis environments is a crucial step in the process of analyzing and dissecting malware and suspicious software. Dynamic analysis allows researchers and cybersecurity professionals to observe the behavior of software in a controlled environment, which is essential for understanding its functionality, detecting malicious activity, and developing effective mitigation strategies.

Dynamic analysis environments are designed to provide a secure and isolated environment where malware samples and potentially harmful software can be executed safely. These environments are crucial because malware often exhibits malicious behavior that can harm a computer system or compromise sensitive data. By conducting dynamic analysis in a controlled setting, analysts can mitigate these risks.

One common approach to setting up a dynamic analysis environment is the use of virtualization technology. Virtualization allows the creation of virtual machines (VMs) that run independently from the host operating system. This isolation ensures that any potentially harmful software executed within a VM does not affect the host system. Popular virtualization platforms like VMware, VirtualBox, and Hyper-V are commonly used for this purpose.

Creating a clean and baseline virtual machine image is an essential step in setting up a dynamic analysis environment. This baseline image serves as a pristine starting point, free from any pre-existing software or configurations that could interfere with the analysis process. Analysts typically install a minimal operating system and essential tools on this clean image.

Snapshotting the baseline image is another crucial aspect of dynamic analysis setup. Snapshots allow analysts to capture the pristine state of the virtual machine at a specific point in time. This snapshot can be reverted to repeatedly, ensuring that the analysis environment is reset to a known good state before each analysis session. This rollback capability is essential for maintaining consistency and repeatability in dynamic analysis.

To conduct dynamic analysis effectively, analysts need a set of tools and utilities that assist in monitoring and capturing the behavior of software during execution. Monitoring tools include process monitors, system activity analyzers, and network traffic capture tools. These tools allow analysts to observe running processes, track system resource usage, and record network communication initiated by the software under analysis.

In addition to monitoring tools, dynamic analysis environments often incorporate sandboxing solutions. Sandboxes are isolated environments where software can be executed safely while being closely monitored. Sandboxing tools, such as Cuckoo Sandbox and VMRay Analyzer, provide automated analysis and behavior tracking capabilities, allowing analysts to assess the impact of malware in a controlled manner.

Network analysis is a critical aspect of dynamic analysis, as malware often communicates with external servers or systems. Network monitoring tools, such as Wireshark and tcpdump, enable analysts to capture and inspect network traffic generated by the software being analyzed. This traffic analysis can reveal command and control communication, data exfiltration, or other suspicious network behavior.

Dynamic analysis environments should also incorporate debugging and memory analysis tools. Debuggers like OllyDbg and WinDbg enable analysts to trace the execution flow of software, set breakpoints, and inspect the state of the system and registers during execution. Memory analysis tools, such as Volatility and Rekall, are essential for inspecting the contents of system memory and identifying the presence of memory-resident malware.

Dynamic analysis environments must be configured to mimic real-world conditions as closely as possible. This includes configuring network settings, DNS resolution, and internet access to resemble the typical environment in which the software operates. Malware often behaves differently in isolation, so accurate network configuration is essential to capture its true behavior.

To maintain the security of the dynamic analysis environment, analysts should implement security measures such as network segmentation. Segmentation isolates the dynamic analysis environment from the production network, preventing potential threats from spreading beyond the controlled environment. Network firewalls and access controls can further enhance security by restricting communication with the outside world.

Dynamic analysis environments must be regularly updated and patched to ensure that the analysis tools and software used within the environment are up to date and free from vulnerabilities. Running outdated software can introduce security risks and compromise the integrity of the analysis process.

Dynamic analysis environments should also have mechanisms in place for handling and storing the results of analysis sessions. Detailed logs and reports should be generated to document the behavior and findings of the analyzed software. These records are valuable for further investigation, reporting, and forensic analysis.

Effective dynamic analysis requires expertise in configuring and maintaining the analysis environment, as well as a deep understanding of the software under investigation. Analysts must be prepared to adapt their environments to suit the specific needs of each analysis session, whether it involves analyzing malware, testing suspicious software, or conducting research on software behavior.

In summary, setting up dynamic analysis environments is a critical step in the process of analyzing and dissecting software for various purposes, including malware analysis, threat detection, and research. These environments provide a controlled and isolated setting where potentially harmful software can be executed safely and monitored closely. By configuring dynamic analysis environments effectively and employing the appropriate tools and techniques, analysts can gain valuable insights into the behavior and functionality of software, enhancing cybersecurity efforts and threat intelligence.

Debugging techniques are essential tools in the arsenal of malware analysts, enabling them to delve deep into the inner workings of malicious software, identify vulnerabilities, and understand its behavior. Debugging allows analysts to step through code, inspect memory, and observe the execution of malware in a controlled environment, ultimately aiding in the development of effective mitigation strategies and threat intelligence.

One of the primary goals of debugging in malware analysis is to gain insight into the malware's functionality by observing its execution step by step. Debuggers are software tools that facilitate this process by allowing analysts to set breakpoints, inspect the state of registers and memory, and trace the execution flow of the malware.

Setting breakpoints is a fundamental debugging technique that enables analysts to pause the execution of malware at specific points in the code. Breakpoints can be placed at critical functions, suspicious code sections, or locations where malware interacts with the system or performs malicious actions. When the malware reaches a breakpoint, it halts execution, allowing analysts to examine the program's state and memory.

Inspecting the state of registers and memory during debugging is crucial for understanding how malware operates. Analysts can examine the contents of CPU registers, stack frames, and memory locations to gain insights into the malware's behavior, data manipulation, and control flow. By observing changes in memory and register values, analysts can identify patterns and uncover the malware's intent.

Tracing the execution flow of malware is another vital aspect of debugging. Analysts use debugger features like single-stepping and instruction tracing to follow the path of execution as the malware progresses through its code. This process helps analysts understand the sequence of actions taken by the malware and can reveal important details about its logic and functionality.

Dynamic analysis and debugging often go hand in hand in the malware analysis process. Dynamic analysis involves executing malware in a controlled environment, while debugging allows analysts to observe and interact with the malware as it runs. Combining these techniques provides a comprehensive view of the malware's behavior and execution, making it easier to identify malicious actions and potential vulnerabilities.

In addition to traditional debugging techniques, malware analysts often encounter obfuscated or anti-analysis code in malicious software. Obfuscation is a common tactic used by malware authors to make their code more difficult to analyze. Obfuscated code may include techniques such as code obfuscation, string encryption, and anti-debugging tricks.

Code obfuscation involves altering the structure and logic of the code to make it less readable and harder to understand. This can include renaming variables, adding unnecessary control flow, and inserting junk instructions. Reverse engineering tools like IDA Pro and Ghidra offer features that help analysts deobfuscate code and restore its original logic.

String encryption is another obfuscation technique used to hide important strings, such as API function names, file paths, and command and control server addresses. Decrypting these strings during analysis is essential to understand the malware's communication and functionality.

Anti-debugging tricks are employed by malware to detect and evade the presence of a debugger. Malware may use various techniques, such as checking for the presence of debugger-specific registry keys or monitoring system interrupts. Analysts must be aware of these anti-debugging mechanisms and use debugger features to bypass or mitigate them.

Memory analysis is closely related to debugging in malware analysis and involves examining the contents of system memory during the execution of malicious code. Memory analysis tools, such as Volatility and Rekall, are invaluable for inspecting the runtime state of malware, identifying injected code, and uncovering rootkits or memory-resident malware.

Malware often injects its code into the address space of legitimate processes to evade detection and analysis. Memory analysis allows analysts to detect these injections, analyze their contents, and understand how they interact with the infected process and the system as a whole.

Exploiting vulnerabilities in malware is a technique used by analysts to gain control over the malware's execution and manipulate its behavior for analysis purposes. By identifying and exploiting vulnerabilities within the malware, analysts can redirect its execution flow, modify its behavior, or extract critical information.

Common vulnerabilities in malware may include buffer overflows, integer overflows, or memory corruption issues. Exploiting these vulnerabilities requires a deep understanding of assembly language and binary analysis, as well as knowledge of the target operating system and architecture.

Another important aspect of debugging techniques in malware analysis is the use of debugging symbols and symbol tables. Debugging symbols are metadata embedded in executable files that provide information about the code, variables, functions, and data structures used in the program. When available, debugging symbols simplify the debugging process by providing meaningful names and labels for code elements.

Debugging symbols are particularly useful when analyzing compiled binaries, as they allow analysts to map assembly code back to high-level source code constructs. This mapping can significantly enhance the understanding of the malware's logic and functionality.

In summary, debugging techniques are essential for malware analysts in their quest to understand and dissect malicious software. These techniques, including setting breakpoints, inspecting registers and memory, tracing execution flow, and exploiting vulnerabilities, empower analysts to gain insights into the malware's behavior and vulnerabilities. Combining dynamic analysis with debugging enables analysts to navigate the complexities of malware, identify malicious actions, and develop effective strategies for threat mitigation and cybersecurity.

Chapter 7: Identifying Malware Behavior Patterns

Behavior analysis is a fundamental approach in the field of cybersecurity and malware detection, providing a crucial line of defense against evolving threats. Unlike signature-based detection methods that rely on known patterns or signatures, behavior analysis focuses on identifying malicious behavior and anomalies exhibited by software and processes, making it a versatile and effective technique in the fight against malware.

The essence of behavior analysis lies in the monitoring and observation of how software, applications, and processes behave during execution. By analyzing their actions and interactions with the system and network, behavior analysis can detect suspicious or unauthorized activities, even when malware employs sophisticated obfuscation techniques to evade detection.

One of the core principles of behavior analysis is the establishment of a baseline of normal behavior for a given system or network. This baseline represents the expected patterns of legitimate software and user activities, allowing security solutions to differentiate between normal and abnormal behavior. Deviations from this baseline are often indicative of malicious activity.

Behavior analysis encompasses a wide range of techniques and methods tailored to various aspects of cybersecurity and malware detection. One common area of focus is network behavior analysis, where the traffic and communication patterns within a network are continuously monitored for anomalies.

Network behavior analysis tools examine network traffic to identify unusual or suspicious activities, such as unexpected data transfers, unusual ports or protocols, and patterns indicative of command and control communication. Detecting these anomalies can help organizations identify potential threats, including malware attempting to exfiltrate data or establish a foothold within the network.

Host-based behavior analysis is another essential component of malware detection, focusing on the behavior of individual systems and endpoints. Host-based behavior analysis solutions monitor processes, system calls, and file activity on a host to identify unusual behavior that may indicate malware infection or malicious activity.

For example, if a legitimate application suddenly exhibits behavior like making unauthorized changes to the registry, modifying system files, or attempting to establish unauthorized network connections, it could be a sign of malware attempting to compromise the system. Behavior analysis tools can raise alerts or take action when such anomalies are detected.

Endpoint detection and response (EDR) solutions leverage behavior analysis to provide real-time visibility into endpoint activity. EDR solutions continuously monitor endpoints for unusual processes, file modifications, and network connections, enabling rapid response to emerging threats. When suspicious behavior is detected, EDR solutions can isolate affected endpoints, contain the threat, and initiate incident response procedures.

User behavior analysis is yet another facet of behavior analysis, focusing on monitoring and analyzing user activities and access patterns. Understanding typical user behavior helps security teams identify anomalies, such as unauthorized access attempts, account compromise, or insider threats. User behavior analysis can assist in detecting malware infections that involve compromised user accounts or insider involvement.

One of the significant advantages of behavior analysis is its adaptability to evolving threats. Unlike signature-based detection, which relies on known patterns of malware, behavior analysis can detect zero-day threats and previously unseen malware. This capability is critical in an ever-changing threat landscape where attackers constantly evolve their tactics and techniques.

Machine learning and artificial intelligence (AI) are increasingly integrated into behavior analysis solutions to enhance their capabilities. These advanced technologies enable behavior analysis tools to learn and adapt to the evolving nature of threats by identifying new patterns of malicious behavior. Machine learning models can analyze vast amounts of data to detect subtle anomalies that may escape traditional detection methods.

Behavior analysis is particularly effective in identifying polymorphic and metamorphic malware, which continuously change their code or appearance to evade signature-based detection. These types of malware often exhibit consistent malicious behavior patterns, making them detectable through behavior analysis even as they alter their code.

Behavior analysis is not limited to detecting malware but also plays a crucial role in identifying other cybersecurity threats, such as advanced persistent threats (APTs), insider threats, and data breaches. By continuously monitoring and analyzing the behavior of systems, networks, and users, organizations can proactively detect and respond to security incidents before they escalate.

In summary, behavior analysis is a key technique in malware detection and cybersecurity, providing a dynamic and adaptable approach to identifying malicious behavior and anomalies. By focusing on the actions and interactions of software, applications, and processes, behavior analysis can detect both known and previously unseen threats, making it an essential component of modern cybersecurity strategies. Leveraging machine learning and AI, behavior analysis solutions can keep pace with the ever-evolving threat landscape, helping organizations protect their systems, data, and networks from a wide range of cyber threats.

Creating behavior profiles is a critical aspect of behavior analysis in cybersecurity and malware detection, allowing organizations to define what constitutes normal behavior for their systems, networks, and users. These profiles serve as a reference point against which deviations and anomalies can be detected and investigated. By establishing comprehensive behavior profiles, organizations can enhance their ability to identify malicious activity and respond effectively to security threats.

Behavior profiles are essentially blueprints that describe the expected behavior of various entities within an organization's IT environment. These entities include individual systems, network devices, applications, and users. Each entity type has its own unique behavior patterns that need to be defined and documented.

System behavior profiles, for example, outline the expected behavior of servers, workstations, and endpoints within an organization's network. These profiles specify typical activities such as system updates, user logins, application launches, and file transfers. Understanding the baseline behavior of systems is essential for identifying deviations that may indicate malware infections or security breaches.

Network behavior profiles describe the expected patterns of network traffic and communication within an organization's network. These profiles encompass normal network protocols, traffic volumes, port usage, and data transfer patterns. Deviations from these profiles can signal malicious network activity, such as unauthorized data exfiltration or lateral movement by an attacker.

Application behavior profiles focus on the expected actions and interactions of software and applications deployed within the organization. This includes how applications access data, communicate with external servers, and interact with the operating system and other applications. Detecting unusual application behavior can help identify potential malware infections or compromised software.

User behavior profiles are crucial for understanding the typical actions and access patterns of individuals within the organization. These profiles encompass user logins, file access, application usage, and network activity. Anomalies in user behavior may indicate compromised user accounts, insider threats, or unauthorized access attempts.

Creating behavior profiles involves a combination of data collection, analysis, and documentation. To establish accurate profiles, organizations must collect data on the behavior of systems, networks, applications, and users over an extended period. This historical data serves as the foundation for understanding what constitutes normal behavior.

Behavior profiles are often defined through a process of data modeling and analysis. Statistical analysis of historical data allows organizations to identify patterns, trends, and outliers. Machine learning and AI technologies can assist in automating this process by identifying significant behavioral features and anomalies.

Documentation is a critical component of behavior profiles, as it ensures that the expected behavior is well-defined and can be communicated effectively across the organization. Profiles should be documented in a clear and accessible manner, making them accessible to security analysts, incident responders, and other stakeholders.

Behavior profiles should be dynamic and adaptable, reflecting changes in the organization's IT environment and threat landscape. As new technologies are adopted, applications are updated, or user roles change, behavior profiles must be adjusted to account for these changes. Regularly updating and fine-tuning behavior profiles is essential for maintaining their effectiveness.

Behavior profiles can be established through a combination of manual and automated processes. Manual profiling involves expert knowledge and analysis of historical data to define expected behavior. Automated profiling, on the other hand, leverages machine learning and AI to discover and adapt to evolving behavioral patterns automatically.

Behavior profiles can also be built through the analysis of known-good data. By examining data from trusted and well-behaved systems, organizations can create templates of normal behavior that can be applied to detect anomalies in other parts of the environment. Known-good data provides a benchmark for identifying deviations.

An important consideration in creating behavior profiles is the differentiation between benign anomalies and malicious activity. Not all deviations from a behavior profile indicate a security threat. Some anomalies may be the result of legitimate changes in the environment, software updates, or user behavior changes. Organizations must have mechanisms in place to assess the severity and potential impact of anomalies.

Behavior profiles serve as the foundation for various cybersecurity and threat detection mechanisms. Intrusion detection systems (IDS) and intrusion prevention systems (IPS) use behavior profiles to identify suspicious network traffic and activities. Security information and event management (SIEM) systems use behavior profiles to correlate and analyze security events across the organization.

User and entity behavior analytics (UEBA) solutions leverage behavior profiles to detect abnormal user actions and potential insider threats. UEBA solutions continuously monitor user behavior, comparing it to established profiles to identify deviations that may indicate compromised accounts or malicious activity.

Behavior-based malware detection systems use behavior profiles to identify malware by analyzing its behavior rather than relying on static signatures. These systems can detect previously unseen malware and zero-day threats by identifying malicious actions or deviations from normal behavior.

In summary, creating behavior profiles is a fundamental step in behavior analysis and cybersecurity, enabling organizations to define and understand the expected behavior of systems, networks, applications, and users. These profiles serve as reference points for identifying anomalies and potential security threats. By continuously monitoring and adapting behavior profiles, organizations can enhance their ability to detect and respond to evolving cybersecurity threats and protect their digital assets.

Chapter 8: Code Deobfuscation and Anti-Analysis Techniques

Dealing with code obfuscation is a fundamental challenge in the field of malware analysis and reverse engineering, as it is a technique employed by malicious actors to obscure the true functionality of their code. Code obfuscation aims to make the analysis and understanding of malware more difficult by transforming the code into a convoluted and less readable form. This practice is prevalent among malware authors who seek to evade detection, hinder reverse engineering efforts, and protect their intellectual property.

Code obfuscation techniques encompass a wide range of strategies, all designed to complicate the analysis process. One common form of obfuscation involves renaming variables, functions, and symbols in the code to obscure their meaning. This makes it challenging for analysts to discern the purpose of specific elements within the code and impedes their ability to understand the program's logic.

Another obfuscation technique involves inserting extraneous code or junk instructions into the program. These additional instructions serve no functional purpose but contribute to the overall complexity of the code, making it more challenging to follow and analyze. The presence of such extraneous code can confuse analysts and consume their time and resources.

String encryption is a prevalent form of obfuscation used to hide important strings within the code, such as API function names, file paths, or command and control server addresses. Malicious actors encrypt these strings to prevent analysts from easily identifying their significance or purpose.

Decrypting these strings during analysis is essential to uncover the malware's communication and functionality.

Control flow obfuscation is another technique employed to confuse the logical flow of the code. It may involve altering the order of instructions, adding conditional branches, or using opaque predicates. These tactics make it difficult for analysts to trace the execution path of the code and understand how different code blocks interact with each other.

Anti-debugging tricks are frequently used in conjunction with code obfuscation to hinder the efforts of analysts attempting to debug the malware. These tricks include checks for the presence of debugger-specific registry keys, monitoring system interrupts, or detecting breakpoints set by the analyst. When anti-debugging mechanisms are triggered, the malware may alter its behavior or terminate to evade analysis.

In the face of code obfuscation, malware analysts employ various strategies to unravel the complexity and reveal the true nature of the malware. One common approach is to employ reverse engineering tools and disassemblers that can assist in deobfuscating the code. Tools like IDA Pro, Ghidra, and OllyDbg offer features specifically designed to help analysts navigate and deobfuscate obfuscated code.

During the analysis process, analysts may manually reverse engineer the obfuscated code by tracing the execution flow, identifying important functions, and mapping out the relationships between different code blocks. This process requires a deep understanding of assembly language and binary analysis, as well as patience and perseverance.

Another effective strategy for dealing with code obfuscation is to leverage debugging and dynamic analysis techniques. Debuggers allow analysts to step through the code, set breakpoints, and inspect the state of the program during execution. By carefully observing the behavior of the malware in a controlled environment, analysts can uncover the true functionality of the obfuscated code.

In some cases, analysts may use code emulation or virtualization techniques to run the malware in an isolated environment where its behavior can be monitored without risk to the host system. This approach can be particularly useful for understanding the malware's actions, interactions with the operating system, and network communication.

Pattern recognition is a valuable tool when dealing with code obfuscation. Analysts can search for recurring patterns or structures within the obfuscated code that may indicate the presence of specific functionality or behavior. Identifying these patterns can provide insights into the malware's logic and functionality.

Collaboration and information sharing among malware analysts and the cybersecurity community are essential when dealing with code obfuscation. Malware analysts often encounter similar obfuscation techniques used across different malware samples. Sharing insights, code snippets, and analysis findings can accelerate the process of deobfuscation and enhance the community's ability to combat obfuscated malware.

Machine learning and artificial intelligence (AI) technologies are increasingly being employed to assist in dealing with code obfuscation. These advanced algorithms can automatically detect and deobfuscate patterns within obfuscated code, aiding analysts in understanding the malware's behavior more quickly and efficiently.

In summary, dealing with code obfuscation is an ongoing challenge in malware analysis and reverse engineering. Malicious actors use a variety of techniques to obscure the true functionality of their code, making it difficult for analysts to understand and combat malware. To overcome these challenges, analysts must employ a combination of reverse engineering tools, debugging techniques, pattern recognition, and collaboration with the cybersecurity community. By unraveling the complexities of obfuscated code, analysts can uncover the true nature of malware and develop effective mitigation strategies.

Overcoming anti-analysis measures is a critical aspect of malware analysis and reverse engineering, as malicious actors employ various techniques to hinder the efforts of analysts and researchers attempting to dissect and understand their malware. These anti-analysis measures are designed to detect the presence of analysis tools, evade debugging, and obstruct the analysis process. Overcoming these obstacles requires a combination of creativity, expertise, and specialized tools and techniques.

One common anti-analysis measure employed by malware authors is the detection of analysis environments. Malware may check for the presence of virtual machines, sandboxes, or debugging tools within the host system. When such tools are detected, the malware may alter its behavior, terminate its execution, or enter a dormant state to avoid detection and analysis.

To overcome this anti-analysis measure, analysts can employ rootkit detection and analysis techniques. Rootkits are malicious software components that hide their presence within a compromised system, making it challenging to detect them. Rootkit detection tools and techniques can help identify and remove rootkits, allowing analysts to analyze the malware without interference.

Malware often employs anti-debugging tricks to detect the presence of a debugger or debugging environment. These tricks include checking for the existence of debugger-specific registry keys, monitoring system interrupts, or inspecting the state of hardware debug registers. When anti-debugging mechanisms are triggered, the malware may behave differently or terminate to thwart analysis.

To overcome anti-debugging measures, analysts can use debugger evasion techniques. These techniques involve setting breakpoints and examining memory in a controlled and stealthy manner to avoid triggering anti-debugging checks. Skilled analysts may also manually modify the malware's code to disable or bypass anti-debugging checks.

Polymorphic and metamorphic malware present a significant challenge in overcoming anti-analysis measures. These types of malware continuously modify their code and appearance to evade detection and analysis. Polymorphic malware generates new code variants with each infection, while metamorphic malware transforms its code each time it executes.

To combat polymorphic and metamorphic malware, analysts may employ techniques such as memory forensics and runtime analysis. Memory forensics tools allow analysts to inspect the contents of system memory during the execution of malware, helping to uncover the runtime-generated code and reveal its true functionality.

Another effective approach to overcoming anti-analysis measures is dynamic analysis within a controlled environment. Dynamic analysis involves executing the malware in an isolated and instrumented environment where its behavior can be closely monitored. This approach allows analysts to observe the malware's actions, interactions with the operating system, and network communication without interference from anti-analysis measures.

Behavior-based analysis and anomaly detection techniques can be valuable in identifying and circumventing anti-analysis measures. By monitoring the behavior of the malware and comparing it to expected patterns, analysts can detect deviations and anomalies that may indicate anti-analysis mechanisms in action. This knowledge can guide further analysis and evasion strategies.

Static analysis tools and techniques can also play a role in overcoming anti-analysis measures. By disassembling and inspecting the code statically, analysts can identify obfuscation techniques, hidden functionality, and anti-analysis mechanisms. Understanding the code's structure and logic can provide insights into how to circumvent these measures. Collaboration within the cybersecurity community is essential when dealing with anti-analysis measures. Malware analysts often encounter similar anti-analysis techniques used across different malware samples. Sharing insights, analysis findings, and evasion strategies can expedite the process of overcoming anti-analysis measures and enhance the community's collective knowledge.

Machine learning and artificial intelligence (AI) technologies are increasingly being leveraged to detect and overcome anti-analysis measures. These advanced algorithms can learn and adapt to the evolving tactics and techniques used by malware authors, helping analysts identify and mitigate anti-analysis mechanisms more effectively.

In summary, overcoming anti-analysis measures is a crucial aspect of malware analysis and reverse engineering. Malicious actors employ various techniques to hinder the efforts of analysts and researchers. To successfully analyze and dissect malware, analysts must employ a combination of creativity, expertise, and specialized tools and techniques. By understanding and circumventing anti-analysis measures, analysts can uncover the true nature of malware and develop effective mitigation strategies to protect systems and networks from cyber threats.

Chapter 9: Reverse Engineering Malicious Network Communication

Analyzing network traffic of malware is a critical aspect of cybersecurity and malware analysis, as it provides valuable insights into the communication and behavior of malicious software. Malware often relies on network communication to receive commands, exfiltrate data, and establish connections to command and control servers, making the analysis of network traffic a key component of understanding and mitigating cyber threats.

The analysis of network traffic begins with the collection of network data, which includes capturing packets, monitoring network logs, and inspecting network flows. Packet capture tools like Wireshark and Tcpdump are commonly used to capture network traffic, allowing analysts to examine the raw data exchanged between systems.

Network logs generated by firewalls, intrusion detection systems (IDS), and other network security appliances provide a wealth of information about network activity, including IP addresses, ports, and protocols. Analyzing these logs can help identify suspicious or anomalous network behavior indicative of malware activity.

Network flow data, which summarizes the characteristics of network traffic over time, can also be instrumental in understanding malware behavior. Flow data includes information about source and destination IP addresses, ports, and the volume of data transferred. Analyzing network flows can reveal patterns and trends in communication.

Once network data is collected, analysts proceed to the examination and analysis phase. This involves dissecting the network traffic to extract relevant information, such as IP addresses, domain names, and communication protocols. Understanding the structure of network packets and protocols is essential for identifying abnormal or malicious behavior.

A critical step in analyzing network traffic is the identification of command and control (C2) communication. Malware often establishes connections to remote C2 servers to receive instructions and transmit stolen data. Detecting C2 communication involves monitoring network traffic for outbound connections to known malicious IP addresses or domains associated with malware infrastructure.

Anomalous network behavior, such as a sudden increase in outbound network traffic or connections to unusual or suspicious IP addresses, can be indicative of malware activity. Identifying these anomalies and correlating them with other indicators of compromise (IOCs) can help pinpoint the presence of malware within a network.

To further analyze network traffic, analysts often employ signature-based detection methods. Signatures are patterns or characteristics that match known malware or attack patterns. Intrusion detection systems (IDS) and security information and event management (SIEM) solutions use signatures to detect and alert on malicious network traffic.

Heuristic and behavioral analysis techniques are also applied to network traffic analysis. Heuristic analysis involves the use of heuristics or rules to identify potential threats based on observed patterns and behaviors. Behavioral analysis focuses on detecting deviations from normal network behavior, which may indicate malicious activity.

Packet inspection and payload analysis are crucial for understanding the content of network traffic. Analysts may inspect the payload of network packets to uncover encoded or encrypted data, which could be indicative of data exfiltration or malicious communication. Decoding and decrypting payload data can provide insights into the malware's objectives and functionality.

Network traffic analysis often involves reverse engineering the communication protocol used by malware. Malicious software may employ custom or proprietary protocols to evade detection. Reverse engineering the protocol allows analysts to understand how the malware communicates, what data it sends and receives, and how it interacts with C2 servers.

Flow analysis and network traffic patterns play a role in identifying lateral movement within a network. Malware may attempt to spread laterally from an infected host to other systems. Analyzing network flows can reveal unusual or unauthorized connections between systems, helping to identify potential lateral movement attempts.

Machine learning and artificial intelligence (AI) are increasingly integrated into network traffic analysis solutions to enhance detection capabilities. These advanced technologies can learn and adapt to evolving malware behavior, making it possible to identify previously unseen threats based on behavioral patterns and anomalies.

Analyzing encrypted network traffic poses a unique challenge for malware analysts. Encrypted communication can hide the content of network packets, making it difficult to inspect payload data for indicators of compromise. To address this challenge, analysts may rely on techniques such as SSL/TLS inspection or network sandboxing to decrypt and analyze encrypted traffic.

In summary, analyzing network traffic of malware is a critical component of cybersecurity and malware analysis. Network data collection, examination, and analysis provide insights into the communication and behavior of malicious software. Detecting command and control communication, identifying anomalies, and applying signature-based, heuristic, and behavioral analysis techniques are essential for uncovering the presence of malware within a network. By leveraging advanced technologies and methodologies, analysts can enhance their ability to detect and respond to cyber threats effectively.

Decrypting and analyzing encrypted communications is a crucial aspect of cybersecurity and digital forensics, as encryption is widely used to protect sensitive information and communications. Malicious actors often employ encryption to conceal their activities and evade detection, making it essential for analysts to possess the knowledge and tools necessary to decrypt and analyze encrypted data.

The process of decrypting and analyzing encrypted communications begins with the identification of encrypted data. Encrypted communications can take various forms, including encrypted files, network traffic secured with protocols like SSL/TLS, and encrypted messages exchanged between individuals or entities. Identifying encrypted data is the first step in understanding the scope of the analysis.

Once encrypted data is identified, analysts must determine the encryption method or algorithm used to secure the data. Different encryption algorithms and techniques require specific decryption approaches. Common encryption algorithms include Advanced Encryption Standard (AES), RSA, and Elliptic Curve Cryptography (ECC). Understanding the encryption method is essential for selecting the appropriate decryption strategy.

One common approach to decrypting encrypted communications involves obtaining the encryption keys or credentials used for encryption. Encryption keys are essential for both encryption and decryption processes, as they determine how data is transformed. Access to the encryption keys can allow analysts to decrypt the data and analyze its content.

Obtaining encryption keys can be challenging, as they are typically stored securely and protected by cryptographic protocols. Malware and cyberattacks may attempt to steal encryption keys, making key management a critical component of encryption security. Analysts may need to use various methods to obtain keys, such as forensic analysis of compromised systems or reverse engineering of malware.

Password-based decryption is another technique employed when encryption keys are not readily available. In this approach, analysts attempt to recover passwords or passphrases used to encrypt data. Passwords can be obtained through various means, including brute-force attacks, dictionary attacks, and the analysis of password hashes.

In cases where encryption keys or passwords are unavailable, analysts may resort to cryptographic attacks to decrypt the data. Cryptographic attacks aim to exploit vulnerabilities in the encryption algorithm or implementation to recover the plaintext. Common cryptographic attacks include chosen plaintext attacks, known plaintext attacks, and padding oracle attacks.

Decryption tools and software can aid analysts in decrypting encrypted communications. These tools are designed to automate the decryption process by leveraging known encryption methods and algorithms. Popular decryption tools include OpenSSL, John the Ripper, and hashcat. Analysts can configure these tools to use dictionary files, wordlists, or custom attack methods to decrypt data.

In cases where the encryption used is weak or flawed, analysts may be able to decrypt the data through cryptographic analysis. Cryptanalysis involves the study of encryption algorithms and their weaknesses to identify vulnerabilities that can be exploited for decryption. Weak key generation, insecure cryptographic implementations, and algorithmic vulnerabilities are common targets for cryptanalysis.

Analyzing encrypted communications requires not only decrypting the data but also examining its content and context. Analysts must understand the purpose of the communication, the parties involved, and the significance of the data being transmitted. Contextual information can provide insights into the nature of the encrypted content and its relevance to the analysis.

Network traffic analysis plays a crucial role in decrypting and analyzing encrypted communications. Encrypted network traffic, such as that secured with SSL/TLS, can be intercepted and decrypted using techniques such as SSL/TLS inspection or man-in-the-middle (MITM) attacks. These approaches allow analysts to inspect the decrypted traffic for indicators of compromise (IOCs) and malicious activity.

Payload analysis is essential for understanding the content of decrypted communications. Payload analysis involves examining the decrypted data to identify sensitive information, malware payloads, or malicious commands. This process may require additional tools and techniques to extract and interpret the decrypted content.

Pattern recognition and signature-based analysis can assist in identifying known threats within decrypted communications. Analysts can compare decrypted data against known threat signatures, IOCs, or attack patterns to detect malicious activity. Signature-based analysis is particularly effective for identifying malware or known attack techniques.

Behavioral analysis is valuable for identifying anomalous or suspicious behavior within decrypted communications. By monitoring the behavior of decrypted data and comparing it to expected patterns, analysts can detect deviations that may indicate malicious activity. Behavioral analysis can uncover unknown threats and zero-day attacks.

Machine learning and artificial intelligence (AI) are increasingly employed in the analysis of encrypted communications. These advanced technologies can automatically classify and analyze decrypted data, detect anomalies, and identify patterns indicative of malicious behavior. Machine learning models can adapt to evolving threats and enhance the accuracy of decryption and analysis.

In summary, decrypting and analyzing encrypted communications is a critical skill in the field of cybersecurity and digital forensics. Understanding encryption methods, obtaining encryption keys or passwords, employing cryptographic attacks, and using decryption tools are essential for decrypting encrypted data. Once decrypted, the analysis of content, context, and behavior can provide valuable insights into the nature of the communication and help detect and mitigate cyber threats effectively. By combining expertise, tools, and techniques, analysts can uncover hidden information and protect systems and networks from malicious actors.

Chapter 10: Malware Reverse Engineering Best Practices and Case Studies

Best practices in malware analysis are essential for conducting effective and thorough examinations of malicious software, ensuring that analysts can understand its functionality, purpose, and potential impact on systems and networks. These practices are critical to the field of cybersecurity and play a pivotal role in identifying and mitigating cyber threats.

One of the fundamental best practices in malware analysis is to perform analysis in a controlled and isolated environment, often referred to as a sandbox or virtual machine. Isolation ensures that the malware does not infect or harm the analyst's system, and it allows for the observation of its behavior without risking the integrity of the host environment.

Creating and maintaining a clean analysis environment is crucial. Analysts should use dedicated systems or virtual machines with no sensitive data or production applications to minimize the risk of contamination. Regularly resetting or reverting the environment to a known-good state ensures that it remains free of artifacts from previous analyses.

Documenting all steps and findings throughout the analysis process is a key best practice. Comprehensive documentation includes recording details such as the malware's file name, hash values, observed behavior, communication patterns, and any indicators of compromise (IOCs) discovered. Proper documentation aids in knowledge sharing, reporting, and future analysis efforts.

Hashing the malware samples is a recommended practice to create unique identifiers for each sample. Hash values, such as MD5, SHA-1, or SHA-256, can be used to reference and compare malware samples. Analysts often share these hash values within the cybersecurity community to facilitate collaboration and threat intelligence sharing.

Taking precautions to avoid network traffic leakage during analysis is essential. Malware may attempt to establish connections or communicate with remote servers. Analysts can use network proxies, sinkholes, or controlled network environments to intercept and monitor this traffic without exposing sensitive data or alerting the malware to the analysis.

Behavior analysis is a core component of malware analysis. Analysts should focus on understanding the actions and interactions of the malware within the analysis environment. This includes monitoring processes, system calls, file system changes, and network activity. Behavioral analysis reveals the malware's intentions and capabilities.

Static analysis, which involves examining the code and structure of the malware without execution, complements behavior analysis. Analysts should disassemble and decompile the malware to gain insights into its logic, functions, and vulnerabilities. Static analysis helps uncover hidden functionality and vulnerabilities.

Using multiple analysis tools and techniques is a recommended practice to enhance the accuracy and completeness of the analysis. Different tools may reveal different aspects of the malware, from code-level details to network communication patterns. Analysts often employ disassemblers, debuggers, hex editors, and dynamic analysis tools to gain a comprehensive understanding.

Reverse engineering skills are essential for in-depth malware analysis. Analysts should possess proficiency in assembly language, binary analysis, and debugging techniques. These skills enable analysts to delve into the intricacies of the malware's code, identify anti-analysis measures, and uncover its inner workings.

Analysts should exercise caution when handling potentially destructive malware. Some malware may contain payloads or triggers that can cause harm or data loss if activated. Isolation and controlled environments are critical for safely analyzing such samples. Additionally, analysts should have backup copies of malware samples to avoid accidental loss or damage.

Maintaining up-to-date knowledge of malware trends, tactics, and techniques is crucial. The threat landscape is continually evolving, and malware authors frequently employ new methods to evade detection and analysis. Analysts must stay informed about the latest threats, malware families, and emerging attack vectors to effectively analyze and mitigate risks.

Collaboration within the cybersecurity community is a best practice that fosters knowledge sharing and threat intelligence exchange. Analysts often encounter similar malware samples or indicators of compromise. Sharing insights, analysis findings, and IOCs with peers and industry groups enhances the collective ability to combat cyber threats.

Malware analysts should follow ethical guidelines and legal requirements when conducting their work. Handling malware samples and communicating findings must adhere to legal and ethical standards. Analysts should be aware of relevant regulations and legal frameworks governing cybersecurity research and investigations.

Effective communication of analysis findings is a best practice to ensure that stakeholders receive actionable information. Analysts should prepare clear and concise reports that highlight the malware's characteristics, behavior, and potential impact. Providing recommendations for remediation and mitigation is essential for helping organizations address the threats identified.

Continuous learning and skill development are essential for staying at the forefront of malware analysis. The field of cybersecurity evolves rapidly, and malware authors continually adapt their tactics. Analysts should invest in training, certifications, and professional development to maintain their expertise and effectiveness.

In summary, best practices in malware analysis are essential for conducting effective and thorough examinations of malicious software. These practices encompass creating isolated analysis environments, documenting findings, hashing samples, avoiding network traffic leakage, performing behavior and static analysis, and using multiple analysis tools and reverse engineering skills. Collaboration, staying informed about the latest threats, ethical conduct, and effective communication are also critical components of best practices in malware analysis. By following these guidelines, analysts can contribute to the detection, analysis, and mitigation of cyber threats effectively.

Real-world case studies in malware reverse engineering provide valuable insights into the practical application of reverse engineering techniques and methodologies. These case studies illustrate how analysts dissect, analyze, and understand the inner workings of actual malware samples encountered in the field of cybersecurity. By examining real-world examples, aspiring and experienced analysts can gain a deeper understanding of the challenges and complexities involved in malware reverse engineering.

One notable case study involves the analysis of the Stuxnet worm, a sophisticated and highly targeted malware that came to light in 2010. Stuxnet was designed to target supervisory control and data acquisition (SCADA) systems, specifically those used in Iran's nuclear program. Analysts discovered that Stuxnet used multiple zero-day vulnerabilities and advanced rootkit techniques to infiltrate and manipulate SCADA systems. Reverse engineering efforts uncovered the worm's complex code, revealing its ability to modify the behavior of industrial controllers. The Stuxnet case study highlights the level of sophistication that can be encountered in real-world malware and the importance of understanding its specific objectives and impact.

Another compelling case study involves the analysis of the Conficker worm, which first emerged in 2008. Conficker was known for its ability to rapidly propagate across vulnerable Windows systems, forming a massive botnet. Reverse engineering efforts focused on understanding how Conficker exploited Windows vulnerabilities and its mechanisms for command and control. The case study demonstrated the importance of timely patching and network segmentation to prevent and mitigate the spread of malware.

The analysis of the WannaCry ransomware outbreak in 2017 serves as a critical case study in understanding the impact of malware on a global scale. WannaCry spread rapidly across unpatched Windows systems, encrypting files and demanding ransom payments in Bitcoin. Reverse engineering efforts revealed the ransomware's encryption algorithm and provided insights into potential decryption methods. The case study emphasized the importance of regular software updates and backups as essential defenses against ransomware attacks.

In the realm of mobile malware, the case study of the Android banking trojan known as Anubis sheds light on the evolving landscape of mobile threats. Anubis targeted Android devices, primarily in the banking sector, and aimed to steal sensitive financial information. Reverse engineering revealed its sophisticated capabilities, including the ability to overlay fake login screens on legitimate banking apps. The case study emphasized the need for mobile device security measures, such as app vetting and user education.

Analyzing the Emotet malware provides insights into the modular nature of modern malware. Emotet, which first appeared in 2014, is a polymorphic banking trojan that evolved into a malware delivery service. Reverse engineering efforts revealed Emotet's modular structure, with various plugins enabling additional functionalities such as spam email distribution and lateral movement within networks. The case study highlighted the adaptability of malware and the importance of analyzing its components comprehensively.

The analysis of the NotPetya ransomware outbreak in 2017 demonstrated the potential for collateral damage in cyberattacks. Initially disguised as ransomware, NotPetya was later revealed to be a wiper malware designed to cause destruction rather than financial gain. Reverse engineering efforts uncovered its propagation methods, including the exploitation of EternalBlue, an exploit stolen from the NSA. The case study underscored the need for robust incident response and recovery strategies in the face of destructive malware.

The case study of the Mirai botnet offers insights into the world of Internet of Things (IoT) malware. Mirai, discovered in 2016, targeted IoT devices and used them to launch distributed denial-of-service (DDoS) attacks. Reverse engineering efforts revealed the botnet's source code, which was subsequently used to create variants targeting additional IoT devices. The case study highlighted the security challenges posed by the proliferation of IoT devices and the importance of securing them against compromise.

Analyzing the TrickBot banking trojan showcases the persistence and adaptability of malware families. TrickBot, initially identified in 2016, evolved to incorporate various modules, including information stealers and ransomware. Reverse engineering efforts have illuminated its command and control infrastructure and communication protocols. The case study emphasized the need for continuous monitoring and threat intelligence to detect and respond to evolving malware threats.

The examination of the Ryuk ransomware illustrates the role of targeted attacks in the ransomware landscape. Ryuk, first observed in 2018, primarily targets organizations with the intent to encrypt their critical data and demand substantial ransoms. Reverse engineering efforts have revealed its encryption mechanisms and tactics for evading detection. The case study emphasized the importance of proactive threat hunting and defense-in-depth strategies in mitigating ransomware threats.

In summary, real-world case studies in malware reverse engineering provide invaluable insights into the ever-evolving landscape of cyber threats. These case studies demonstrate the sophistication, diversity, and impact of malware encountered in the field of cybersecurity. Through reverse engineering efforts, analysts uncover the inner workings of malware, its propagation methods, and its specific objectives. By studying real-world examples, cybersecurity professionals can enhance their skills and knowledge to better defend against emerging threats and protect systems and networks from malicious actors.

BOOK 2
MASTERING MALWARE REVERSE ENGINEERING
FROM NOVICE TO EXPERT

ROB BOTWRIGHT

Chapter 1: Building a Strong Foundation in Malware Analysis

Understanding malware types is essential for anyone involved in cybersecurity, as it forms the foundation for recognizing, analyzing, and mitigating cyber threats. Malware, short for malicious software, encompasses a broad spectrum of malicious programs and code designed to compromise, damage, or control computer systems and networks. One of the most common types of malware is viruses, which are self-replicating programs that attach themselves to legitimate files or programs and spread when these files are executed. Viruses often modify or corrupt files and can lead to system instability and data loss.

Worms are another prevalent type of malware, distinguished by their ability to self-replicate and spread independently without the need for user intervention. Worms can rapidly propagate across networks, infecting multiple systems and causing congestion and disruption. Trojan horses, often referred to as Trojans, disguise themselves as legitimate software or files to deceive users into executing them. Once activated, Trojans can perform a wide range of malicious actions, such as stealing sensitive data, creating backdoors, or facilitating remote control by attackers.

Ransomware is a particularly destructive type of malware that encrypts a victim's files or system and demands a ransom for the decryption key. Victims are often coerced into paying the ransom to regain access to their data, making ransomware a financially motivated threat.

Spyware is designed to monitor and gather information from infected systems without the user's knowledge or consent. It can capture keystrokes, record browsing habits, and steal sensitive data, posing significant privacy and security risks.

Adware, while less harmful than other malware types, can be intrusive and disruptive by displaying unwanted advertisements and redirecting web traffic. Adware often accompanies legitimate software installations, making it challenging to avoid.

Rootkits are stealthy malware that aim to gain unauthorized access to a system, establish persistent control, and hide their presence from security tools and users. Rootkits can be challenging to detect and remove.

Keyloggers are a subset of spyware that focus specifically on recording keystrokes. These malicious programs are often used to capture passwords, login credentials, and other sensitive information.

Botnets consist of compromised computers, or "bots," that are controlled remotely by a central command and control server. Botnets can be used for various purposes, including launching DDoS attacks, sending spam emails, and distributing malware.

Fileless malware is a relatively new type of malware that operates in memory, leaving no traditional traces on disk. Fileless malware leverages scripting languages and legitimate system processes to carry out malicious actions, making it challenging to detect.

Polymorphic and metamorphic malware are known for their ability to change their code or appearance with each infection, evading signature-based detection methods. These malware types pose significant challenges for traditional antivirus solutions.

Multipartite malware combines features of multiple malware types, making them versatile and difficult to remove. Multipartite malware may use a combination of viruses, Trojans, and worms to infect and spread.

Macro malware leverages macros in documents and spreadsheets to execute malicious code when the document is opened. Macro malware often arrives as email attachments or downloads from malicious websites.

Mobile malware targets smartphones and tablets, seeking to compromise mobile operating systems and applications. Mobile malware can steal personal data, send premium-rate SMS messages, and gain unauthorized access to device functions.

Rogue security software, commonly referred to as "scareware" or "fake antivirus," tricks users into believing their systems are infected and prompts them to purchase bogus security software. Rogue security software does not provide actual protection and can lead to financial loss.

File infector malware modifies executable files, infecting them with malicious code that can be executed when the infected file is run. File infector malware can compromise the integrity of system files and applications.

Memory-resident malware operates in a system's memory and does not rely on files or disk storage. Memory-resident malware can be challenging to detect, as it does not leave persistent traces on the system.

Macro viruses target macros in documents and spreadsheets, infecting these files and spreading when they are opened. Macro viruses were more prevalent in the past but still pose a threat in certain scenarios.

Browser hijackers take control of a user's web browser, altering its settings, redirecting web traffic, and displaying unwanted ads. Browser hijackers can negatively impact the browsing experience.

Malvertising involves the use of malicious online advertisements to deliver malware to users' devices. Malvertisements can exploit vulnerabilities in web browsers or plugins, leading to malware infections.

Understanding the characteristics, behavior, and objectives of various malware types is crucial for effective cybersecurity. Each type of malware presents unique challenges and requires specific countermeasures and analysis techniques. By staying informed about the latest malware trends and threats, cybersecurity professionals can better protect systems and networks from evolving cyberattacks. Essential malware analysis tools are the cornerstone of any effective malware analysis process, enabling analysts to dissect, understand, and mitigate malicious software. These tools encompass a wide range of applications and utilities designed to aid in various aspects of malware analysis, from static and dynamic analysis to reverse engineering and behavioral profiling.

A fundamental tool in the arsenal of malware analysts is the disassembler, which allows them to convert compiled binary code into human-readable assembly language. Popular disassemblers such as IDA Pro and Ghidra enable analysts to examine the inner workings of malware, identify functions, and understand the flow of code execution.

Dynamic analysis tools play a crucial role in observing malware behavior during runtime. Sandboxes, such as Cuckoo Sandbox and Joe Sandbox, create isolated environments where malware can be executed safely, enabling analysts to monitor its actions, file changes, network communications, and system modifications.

Debuggers are essential for live debugging and analysis of malware samples. Tools like OllyDbg, WinDbg, and Immunity Debugger allow analysts to set breakpoints, inspect memory, and step through code execution, providing insights into how malware operates and making it possible to identify vulnerabilities.

Hex editors and binary file viewers are invaluable for examining the raw binary data of malware files. These tools, such as HxD and 010 Editor, enable analysts to view and edit binary data, search for specific patterns, and uncover hidden information within malware samples.

Memory analysis tools, like Volatility and Rekall, focus on analyzing the contents of a system's memory. Memory forensics is essential for identifying malware artifacts that may not be present in disk-based analysis, such as injected code, rootkits, and active processes.

Packet capture and analysis tools, such as Wireshark and tcpdump, are crucial for inspecting network traffic generated by malware. Analysts can use these tools to capture, analyze, and decode network packets, uncovering communication patterns, command and control channels, and data exfiltration. YARA is a powerful tool for creating and applying custom rules to identify specific patterns or characteristics within malware samples. Analysts can write YARA rules to detect known malware families, file signatures, or behaviors, aiding in the identification and classification of malware.

Anti-debugging and anti-analysis tools are used by malware authors to hinder analysis efforts. Malware analysts may employ tools like x64dbg and Scylla to bypass anti-debugging techniques and recover control over the analysis process.

Binary and file format analysis tools assist in understanding the structure and format of executable files and data files. Tools like PE Explorer and FileInsight enable analysts to inspect headers, sections, and metadata within binary files.

In-depth network traffic analysis tools, such as Suricata and Snort, are essential for monitoring and detecting network-based threats. These intrusion detection systems (IDS) can analyze network packets in real-time, alerting analysts to suspicious or malicious activities.

Static analysis tools automate the examination of malware samples without executing them. These tools, including PEiD and PEStudio, inspect file headers, import/export tables, and strings, providing insights into file characteristics and potential malicious indicators. Code deobfuscation and unpacking tools help analysts reverse the obfuscation techniques used by malware authors to hide their code. Tools like x64dbg, OllyDump, and unpackers specific to malware families can assist in revealing the original code.

Behavioral analysis tools, such as RegShot and Process Monitor, track system changes caused by malware execution. These tools create logs of registry modifications, file creations, and process activities, allowing analysts to identify malicious actions. Network traffic capture and analysis tools, such as Bro and Zeek, enable analysts to monitor network traffic and extract useful information, such as IP addresses, domain names, and communication protocols, for further analysis. Anti-reverse engineering tools, like Themida and VMProtect, are used by software developers to protect their applications from analysis and reverse engineering. Analysts may need to overcome these protections to analyze malware effectively. File extraction and decompression tools, such as 7-Zip and WinRAR, are essential for extracting and examining the contents of compressed or archived files within malware samples.

Scripting languages, such as Python and PowerShell, are valuable for automation and custom analysis scripts. Analysts can create scripts to parse and process data, automate repetitive tasks, and enhance their analysis workflows. Code analysis frameworks, like Angr and Triton, provide advanced capabilities for symbolic execution and program analysis. These frameworks are used for in-depth analysis of complex malware samples and vulnerability discovery.

Memory dump analysis tools, such as Volatility and Rekall, are crucial for analyzing memory dumps acquired from compromised systems. These tools aid in the extraction of artifacts, processes, and network connections from memory. Malware analysis platforms, such as REMnux and FLARE VM, offer pre-configured environments with a collection of analysis tools and utilities, simplifying the setup and preparation for malware analysis tasks.

Collaboration and information sharing tools, such as VirusTotal and Hybrid Analysis, allow analysts to submit and query malware samples against extensive databases, benefiting from collective intelligence and threat intelligence feeds.

Dynamic analysis tools, such as Procmon and ApateDNS, assist in monitoring system activity and DNS resolution during malware execution, aiding in the identification of malicious behavior.

String analysis tools, like Strings and BinText, help analysts extract and examine strings within malware binaries, revealing valuable information such as URLs, API calls, and embedded commands.

Machine learning and AI-based tools, such as those integrated into modern security solutions, can aid in automating malware detection and analysis, improving the efficiency of threat detection and response.

In summary, essential malware analysis tools are indispensable for cybersecurity professionals engaged in the detection, analysis, and mitigation of malicious software. These tools encompass a wide range of functionalities, including disassembling, debugging, memory analysis, network traffic monitoring, and behavior tracking. By mastering the use of these tools and leveraging their capabilities, analysts can effectively uncover and combat the ever-evolving landscape of cyber threats.

Chapter 2: Advanced Assembly Language and Code Analysis

Mastering assembly language instructions is a critical skill for malware analysts, reverse engineers, and cybersecurity professionals, as it forms the foundation for understanding the low-level operations of a computer's central processing unit (CPU). Assembly language, often referred to as assembly code, provides a human-readable representation of machine code instructions, allowing analysts to examine and manipulate binary programs at the most granular level.

Assembly language instructions are specific commands that correspond to individual operations performed by the CPU. These instructions are expressed in a mnemonic format, making it easier for humans to comprehend and work with machine code. Each assembly instruction typically consists of an opcode (operation code) and operands, which specify the data or registers involved in the operation.

The x86 architecture is one of the most widely used CPU architectures in the world and is frequently encountered in malware analysis and reverse engineering tasks. Learning x86 assembly language instructions is a fundamental step in mastering assembly language, as it provides a solid foundation for understanding other assembly languages used in various CPU architectures.

One of the essential assembly instructions in x86 is the "MOV" instruction, which stands for "move." The MOV instruction is used to transfer data from one location to another, such as from memory to a register or between registers. Understanding how to use the MOV instruction is crucial for manipulating and examining data within a program.

Another fundamental assembly instruction is the "ADD" instruction, which is used for addition operations. The ADD instruction adds two values and stores the result in a specified destination operand. This instruction is vital for performing arithmetic operations and calculations within a program.

The "SUB" instruction, short for "subtract," is used to perform subtraction operations. It subtracts one value from another and stores the result in the destination operand. Subtraction operations are common in mathematical calculations and data manipulation.

Conditional branch instructions are essential for controlling the flow of a program based on specific conditions. Instructions like "JZ" (jump if zero) and "JNZ" (jump if not zero) allow programs to make decisions and execute different code paths depending on the outcome of previous operations. Conditional branches are critical for implementing loops and branching logic in assembly code.

The "CMP" instruction, which stands for "compare," is often used in conjunction with conditional branches. The CMP instruction compares two values and sets the CPU's status flags (such as the zero flag and sign flag) based on the result of the comparison. These flags are then used by conditional branch instructions to determine the program's flow.

Memory access instructions, such as "MOV" and "LEA" (load effective address), are crucial for reading from and writing to memory locations. Memory access instructions allow programs to store and retrieve data from memory, making them essential for data manipulation and storage.

The "CALL" and "RET" (return) instructions are used for function calls and returns in assembly language. These instructions enable programs to call subroutines or functions and return control to the calling code. Proper use of CALL and RET instructions is essential for program organization and modularity.

The "PUSH" and "POP" instructions are used to manipulate the stack, a critical data structure in assembly language. The PUSH instruction pushes a value onto the stack, while the POP instruction removes and retrieves a value from the stack. The stack is commonly used for function call management and storing temporary data.

Logical operations, including "AND," "OR," and "XOR," are essential for performing bitwise operations on data. These instructions enable programs to manipulate individual bits within binary data, making them valuable for tasks like data encryption and manipulation.

Shift and rotate instructions, such as "SHL" (shift left) and "ROR" (rotate right), are used to shift or rotate bits within a binary value. These instructions are valuable for tasks like data manipulation and bit-level operations.

The "INC" (increment) and "DEC" (decrement) instructions are used to increase or decrease the value of a register or memory location by one. These instructions are commonly used in loops and counter operations.

Floating-point instructions, such as "FADD" (floating-point addition) and "FMUL" (floating-point multiplication), are essential for performing mathematical operations on floating-point numbers. Floating-point instructions are used in scientific and engineering applications that require high precision.

String instructions, like "MOVSB" (move string byte) and "SCASB" (scan string for byte), are used for manipulating and searching strings of data in memory. These instructions are valuable for tasks involving text processing and data analysis.

Understanding assembly language instructions involves mastering their syntax, operands, and the effects they have on the CPU's registers and memory. Analysts must become proficient in reading and writing assembly code, as well as interpreting the logic and flow of programs at the assembly level.

Practical experience and hands-on exercises are crucial for gaining proficiency in assembly language instructions. Analysts should practice writing and analyzing assembly code to become comfortable with the nuances of different instructions and their interactions within programs.

In summary, mastering assembly language instructions is a fundamental skill for malware analysts, reverse engineers, and cybersecurity professionals. These instructions provide insight into the low-level operations of computer programs, enabling analysts to dissect and understand binary code. Whether working with x86 architecture or other CPU architectures, a deep understanding of assembly language instructions is essential for effective malware analysis and reverse engineering.

Advanced code analysis techniques are an indispensable aspect of malware analysis and reverse engineering, enabling analysts to delve deeper into the intricacies of malicious software and uncover hidden functionalities. These techniques go beyond basic static and dynamic analysis, providing a more comprehensive understanding of the code's behavior, obfuscation mechanisms, and evasion tactics employed by malware authors.

One advanced code analysis technique involves unpacking and decrypting malware payloads. Many malware samples use packing or encryption to conceal their malicious code and evade detection. Analysts use various methods, including debugging and memory analysis, to identify and extract the original code hidden within packed or encrypted sections. Unpacking malware is a critical step in understanding its functionality and behavior.

Another advanced technique is the analysis of code injection and hooking mechanisms. Malware often injects its code into legitimate processes or hooks system functions to gain control over a system. Analysts use debugging and tracing tools to track the execution flow of injected code, identifying its purpose and any malicious actions it performs within the compromised system.

Code deobfuscation is a vital technique for reversing obfuscated and encrypted code within malware samples. Obfuscation is commonly employed to make reverse engineering more challenging. Analysts use specialized tools and custom scripts to deobfuscate code, making it readable and easier to analyze. Deobfuscation allows analysts to understand the malware's logic and intentions.

Advanced code analysis also involves examining anti-reverse engineering techniques employed by malware authors. Malware may include anti-debugging, anti-analysis, or anti-VM (virtual machine) measures to hinder analysis efforts. Analysts employ creative debugging strategies, such as modifying CPU flags and memory breakpoints, to bypass these protections and gain control over the code execution.

Behavioral analysis is an advanced technique that involves tracking and analyzing the runtime behavior of malware. While traditional dynamic analysis focuses on monitoring system calls and network traffic, behavioral analysis dives deeper into understanding the malware's actions within the system, including file manipulation, registry modifications, and process interactions. This technique provides insights into the malware's objectives and potential impact.

Memory forensics is another advanced technique used to analyze a system's memory for artifacts left by malware. Analysts employ memory analysis tools to extract information about running processes, loaded modules, and network connections from a system's RAM. Memory forensics is invaluable for identifying hidden malware components and uncovering evidence of malicious activities. Reverse engineering malware communication protocols is an advanced technique used to dissect the methods by which malware communicates with command and control (C2) servers. Analysts capture and analyze network traffic to understand the protocols, encryption, and data exchanged between the malware and C2 servers. This analysis helps in identifying the malware's control infrastructure and the data it exfiltrates or receives.

Advanced code analysis often involves the study of evasion tactics used by malware to avoid detection by security tools and sandboxes. This includes examining techniques such as sandbox detection, timing-based evasion, and environmental checks. Analysts devise countermeasures and modify the execution environment to prevent these evasion techniques from succeeding.

Behavior pattern analysis is a sophisticated technique that involves identifying patterns and heuristics in malware behavior. Analysts develop behavioral profiles of malware families or categories based on observed actions and sequences of events. This technique aids in the automated detection and classification of malware based on its behavior, even when it employs polymorphism or changes its code.

Code emulation and instrumentation are advanced techniques used to dynamically analyze malware samples within controlled environments. Analysts create custom emulators or instrument existing ones to execute and monitor malware behavior. Emulation and instrumentation enable deep inspection of code execution and data flows, facilitating comprehensive analysis.

Code graph analysis is an advanced technique that visualizes the relationships between functions and control flows within a malware binary. Analysts use tools like IDA Pro and Ghidra to create code graphs, allowing them to navigate and understand complex code structures more efficiently. Code graph analysis aids in identifying critical functions and code paths within malware.

Rootkit analysis is an advanced area of research focusing on detecting and analyzing rootkits, which are malicious software components that conceal their presence and control over a compromised system. Analysts use kernel-level debugging and forensic techniques to uncover rootkit artifacts and understand their mechanisms for maintaining persistence and stealth.

Advanced code analysis techniques often involve the identification and exploitation of vulnerabilities within malware. Analysts search for weaknesses or flaws in the code that can be leveraged to disrupt the malware's operations or mitigate its impact. Vulnerability analysis is essential for developing countermeasures and protective measures against malware threats.

In summary, advanced code analysis techniques are essential for in-depth malware analysis and reverse engineering. These techniques empower analysts to unpack, deobfuscate, and understand the inner workings of malware, even in the presence of evasion and anti-analysis measures. By employing advanced methods, cybersecurity professionals gain the expertise needed to effectively combat sophisticated and evolving malware threats.

Chapter 3: Dynamic Analysis and Advanced Debugging Techniques

Dynamic analysis tools and their proper setup are fundamental components of malware analysis and reverse engineering, allowing analysts to observe and understand how malicious software behaves during runtime. Dynamic analysis provides valuable insights into a malware sample's execution, including its interactions with the host system, network communications, and the impact it may have on compromised systems.

Dynamic analysis begins with the selection and configuration of a suitable analysis environment. Analysts often use virtual machines (VMs) to create isolated and controlled environments for executing malware samples safely. These VMs are set up to mimic target operating systems and configurations, providing a controlled environment for analysis.

Before executing a malware sample in the analysis environment, it is essential to prepare the VM by taking snapshots or creating a baseline image. This allows analysts to revert the VM to a clean state after each analysis session, ensuring that any changes made by the malware do not persist or affect subsequent analyses.

Dynamic analysis tools encompass a wide range of utilities designed to monitor and capture various aspects of a malware's behavior. One fundamental tool is the debugger, which allows analysts to observe and control the execution of the malware at the assembly code level. Popular debuggers like OllyDbg, WinDbg, and Immunity Debugger provide capabilities for setting breakpoints, inspecting registers and memory, and stepping through code execution.

Process monitoring tools, such as Process Monitor (Procmon) and Process Explorer, are essential for tracking changes made by malware within the system. These tools log file system activity, registry modifications, and process creation, helping analysts understand the malware's impact on the host system.

Packet capture tools, like Wireshark and tcpdump, are used to intercept and record network traffic generated by the malware. Analysts configure these tools to capture traffic on the virtual network interface of the analysis environment, allowing them to monitor outbound and inbound communications.

Dynamic analysis environments are often equipped with network analysis tools like Snort and Suricata, which function as intrusion detection systems (IDS). These tools can detect and alert analysts to suspicious network activity, such as known attack patterns or malicious traffic generated by the malware.

Memory analysis tools, such as Volatility and Rekall, are crucial for examining the contents of the system's RAM during runtime. Memory forensics enables analysts to identify running processes, loaded modules, and network connections established by the malware, providing insights into its behavior.

Sandboxing solutions, such as Cuckoo Sandbox and Joe Sandbox, offer automated dynamic analysis by executing malware samples in controlled environments and generating comprehensive reports. Analysts submit malware samples to these sandboxes, which record system activity, network communication, and file changes, facilitating quick analysis.

Dynamic analysis tools often include debuggers with additional features for analyzing malware behavior. For example, dynamic analysis debuggers may have scripting capabilities that enable analysts to automate tasks, extract data, and perform custom analysis routines.

Runtime analysis tools can monitor the behavior of a malware sample as it interacts with the operating system's APIs (Application Programming Interfaces). These tools provide visibility into API calls made by the malware, helping analysts understand its actions and intentions.

Behavioral profiling tools, such as RegShot and API Monitor, capture changes made to the system's configuration, registry, and files during malware execution. This information aids in understanding the malware's persistence mechanisms and system modifications.

Dynamic analysis tools also encompass network emulation environments, such as INetSim and Honeyd, which simulate network services and responses. These tools trick malware into thinking it is communicating with real servers and services, allowing analysts to observe network behaviors without exposing the analysis environment to real-world risks.

When setting up a dynamic analysis environment, analysts must consider the network configuration. Isolating the analysis environment from the production network is crucial to prevent accidental network attacks or unwanted communication with external entities.

To ensure accurate analysis results, analysts often use a variety of network configuration techniques, including network address translation (NAT) and firewalls, to control and monitor network traffic between the analysis environment and external systems.

Dynamic analysis tools should be updated regularly to ensure compatibility with the latest malware threats and operating system updates. Analysts must keep their toolsets current to effectively analyze new and evolving malware samples.

It is also essential to establish proper logging and monitoring within the dynamic analysis environment. Detailed logs of system activities, network traffic, and process executions should be generated and preserved for future reference and analysis.

During the dynamic analysis process, analysts must exercise caution to prevent accidental contamination of their analysis environment. Malware may attempt to propagate, self-replicate, or spread to other systems if not contained properly.

As part of the analysis workflow, analysts often use virtual private networks (VPNs) to route the analysis environment's network traffic through secure channels. This minimizes the risk of exposing the analysis environment to external threats and provides a layer of protection.

Another aspect of dynamic analysis setup involves the use of decoy or honeypot systems. Decoy systems are intentionally vulnerable machines that mimic potential targets for the malware. Analysts can use decoys to divert malware activity away from critical systems, allowing them to observe the malware's behavior without risking damage to real assets.

Dynamic analysis tools and setup require careful planning and consideration to ensure accurate and comprehensive malware analysis. Analysts must choose the appropriate tools, configure the analysis environment securely, and implement monitoring and containment measures to protect their systems and network during the analysis process. Properly executed dynamic analysis provides invaluable insights into malware behavior, enabling analysts to develop effective countermeasures and enhance cybersecurity defenses.

Advanced debugging strategies are indispensable for malware analysts, reverse engineers, and software developers seeking to unravel complex code, identify vulnerabilities, and gain deep insights into program behavior. These strategies go beyond basic debugging techniques, offering a toolbox of advanced approaches to troubleshoot and analyze intricate software systems effectively.

One fundamental advanced debugging technique is conditional breakpoints. Conditional breakpoints allow developers and analysts to pause program execution only when specific conditions or expressions evaluate to true. This enables pinpoint debugging, focusing on critical code paths or specific states within the program.

Another powerful strategy is the use of tracepoints. Tracepoints are dynamic debugging markers that record program events or variable values without interrupting execution. Analysts can strategically place tracepoints to capture data at specific points in the code, providing a comprehensive view of program behavior.

Dynamic analysis and debugging techniques involve runtime inspection of programs. Dynamic analysis tools, such as memory profilers and code instrumentation, enable analysts to track memory usage, resource allocation, and execution flows during program execution. This real-time insight is invaluable for identifying memory leaks, performance bottlenecks, and unexpected behaviors.

API-level debugging allows analysts to intercept and modify system calls and application programming interface (API) functions during execution. This strategy is particularly useful for tracing interactions with the operating system, identifying malicious behavior, and understanding how malware interfaces with system components.

Advanced debugging often involves the use of memory analysis tools, such as memory dump analysis and heap debugging. Memory analysis tools help uncover memory-related issues, buffer overflows, and memory corruption vulnerabilities. Analysts can inspect memory dumps to diagnose crashes and examine memory structures.

Kernel-mode debugging is a specialized technique used for debugging kernel-level code and device drivers. Kernel debuggers, like WinDbg and GDB, enable analysts to inspect and manipulate the kernel's execution, making it possible to identify and resolve issues related to device drivers or system stability.

An important aspect of advanced debugging is the analysis of multithreaded and concurrent programs. Multithreaded debugging tools assist in tracking thread synchronization, race conditions, and deadlock scenarios. Detecting and resolving concurrency-related issues is crucial for improving program reliability and performance.

Reversing and debugging packed or obfuscated code is a challenging but essential aspect of advanced debugging. Analysts use specialized debuggers, unpackers, and deobfuscation techniques to reveal the original code hidden within packed or obfuscated binaries. This process is vital for understanding malware behavior and uncovering evasion tactics.

Memory forensics is a technique that involves analyzing memory dumps or snapshots to investigate system compromises and malware infections. Memory forensics tools, such as Volatility and Rekall, help analysts extract valuable artifacts, such as running processes, loaded modules, and network connections, from memory.

Fault injection and fuzzing are proactive debugging strategies used to identify vulnerabilities and weaknesses in software. Analysts inject faults, such as invalid inputs or unexpected conditions, into programs to observe their responses and trigger potential crashes or vulnerabilities.

Runtime code analysis tools, including dynamic binary instrumentation frameworks like Pin and DynamoRIO, enable deep inspection of program execution. Analysts can instrument code at runtime, monitor function calls, and trace program flows to gain insights into complex code paths.

Live debugging is a strategy employed to analyze and diagnose issues in real-time, often in production environments. Live debugging tools, such as remote debugging and attachable debuggers, allow analysts to connect to running processes and inspect their state without disrupting system operation.

Distributed systems debugging focuses on identifying and resolving issues within distributed software systems and microservices architectures. Debugging distributed systems involves tracing message flows, tracking latency, and analyzing interactions among distributed components.

Advanced debugging strategies often require the use of custom scripts and automation. Analysts develop scripts to automate debugging tasks, collect data, and perform repetitive actions, streamlining the debugging process and improving efficiency.

Machine learning-based debugging tools and anomaly detection techniques are emerging as advanced strategies for identifying unusual program behavior and deviations from expected norms. These tools can help analysts quickly pinpoint and address abnormal patterns and security incidents.

Debugging in production environments poses unique challenges, as errors or crashes can impact users. Advanced debugging techniques for production systems involve log analysis, telemetry data collection, and canary releases to isolate issues and minimize downtime.

Advanced debugging strategies also encompass the analysis of crash dumps and core dumps generated when a program crashes. These dumps contain valuable information, such as the call stack, registers, and memory contents at the time of the crash, aiding in root cause analysis.

Advanced debugging often involves analyzing and debugging complex data structures, including linked lists, trees, and graphs. Specialized data structure visualization tools assist analysts in understanding the organization and relationships within these data structures.

Reverse debugging is an innovative technique that allows analysts to step backward in program execution, effectively "rewinding" the program's behavior to identify the origin of a problem or error. This approach is particularly valuable for troubleshooting intermittent or hard-to-reproduce issues.

When dealing with remote or cloud-based applications, remote debugging techniques enable analysts to debug code running on remote servers or virtual machines. Remote debugging tools facilitate collaboration and troubleshooting in distributed environments.

Advanced debugging strategies extend beyond traditional debugging tools and methodologies, requiring a deep understanding of program internals, system architecture, and software behavior. These techniques empower analysts to tackle complex issues, uncover vulnerabilities, and enhance the reliability and security of software systems.

Chapter 4: Unpacking and Decrypting Malicious Payloads

Unpacking malware is a critical process in the realm of malware analysis and reverse engineering, as many malicious programs employ packing techniques to evade detection and analysis. Packing is the process of compressing and encrypting the executable code of a malware sample to make it more challenging to analyze and detect by security solutions.

To effectively unpack malware, analysts must employ a variety of techniques and tools to reveal the original, unpacked code hidden within the packed binary.

One common technique for unpacking malware is dynamic analysis. In dynamic analysis, analysts execute the packed malware within a controlled environment, such as a virtual machine, and monitor its behavior during runtime. Dynamic analysis allows analysts to observe the unpacking process as the malware decrypts its code and begins executing.

During dynamic analysis, analysts may employ debugger tools to pause the malware's execution at specific points of interest, such as before and after the unpacking routine. This enables them to inspect memory and registers to capture the unpacked code and any decrypted data.

Another useful approach is memory analysis, which involves examining the contents of the system's RAM during malware execution. Memory analysis tools, such as Volatility or Rekall, allow analysts to identify processes associated with the malware and extract unpacked code and data directly from memory.

String analysis is a valuable technique for identifying indicators of the unpacked code within the packed binary. Analysts can search for known strings or signatures that are characteristic of the malware's unpacked code, helping to pinpoint the location of the unpacked code within the binary.

Advanced unpacking techniques may involve using custom scripts or tools to automate the unpacking process. Analysts may write scripts that simulate the malware's execution, allowing them to trace the unpacking routine step by step and capture the unpacked code as it becomes accessible in memory.

Emulation environments, such as QEMU or Bochs, can be employed to simulate the execution of the packed malware. Emulators allow analysts to execute the packed binary while monitoring its interactions with the emulated environment, facilitating the unpacking process.

Static analysis techniques can also aid in unpacking malware. Analysts may disassemble the packed binary using tools like IDA Pro or Ghidra to analyze the unpacking routine and understand how it decrypts and unpacks the code.

Pattern recognition is a technique that involves identifying known packing algorithms or encryption methods used by the malware. Analysts can create custom scripts or tools to recognize patterns in the binary's structure or behavior that indicate the presence of packing routines.

Signature-based detection can be employed to identify known packers or encryption algorithms used by the malware. Analysts can compare the binary's characteristics to a database of known packer signatures to determine the type of packing used.

In some cases, unpacking malware may require reverse engineering the packing algorithm itself. Analysts may need to analyze the malware's packing routine and develop custom tools or scripts to decrypt and unpack the code manually.

Dynamic debugging techniques can aid in unpacking malware by allowing analysts to step through the unpacking routine and monitor memory and register changes in real-time. Debuggers like OllyDbg or WinDbg can be used for this purpose.

Behavioral analysis can provide valuable insights into the unpacking process. Analysts can observe how the packed malware interacts with the system and external resources during execution, helping to understand the unpacking routine's behavior.

Unpacking malware is a complex and iterative process that often requires a combination of techniques and tools. Analysts must be persistent and creative in their approach, as malware authors continuously develop new packing and obfuscation methods to evade analysis.

Moreover, unpacking malware requires a deep understanding of assembly language, as analysts must be able to navigate and interpret the disassembled code to identify the unpacking routine and its key components.

Successful unpacking of malware is a crucial step in the analysis process, as it reveals the malware's true capabilities and behavior, enabling analysts to develop effective countermeasures and protections against the threat.

Decrypting encrypted payloads is a complex but essential task in malware analysis and reverse engineering, as many malicious programs employ encryption techniques to conceal their true functionality and evade detection. Encryption is the process of encoding data in a way that makes it unreadable without the corresponding decryption key, and malware often uses encryption to protect sensitive components of its code or data.

To effectively decrypt encrypted payloads, analysts must employ various techniques and tools to reverse the encryption process and reveal the original, unencrypted content.

One common technique for decrypting encrypted payloads is dynamic analysis. During dynamic analysis, analysts execute the malware that contains the encrypted payload within a controlled environment, such as a virtual machine, and monitor its behavior during runtime. Dynamic analysis allows analysts to observe how the malware uses encryption keys and algorithms to decrypt the payload and access its contents.

Debugger tools can be valuable during dynamic analysis, as they enable analysts to pause the malware's execution at critical points where decryption occurs. Analysts can inspect the memory and registers at these points to capture the decrypted payload as it becomes accessible during runtime.

Memory analysis techniques can also aid in decrypting encrypted payloads. Memory analysis tools, such as Volatility or Rekall, allow analysts to examine the contents of the system's RAM during malware execution. By analyzing memory dumps, analysts can identify processes, memory regions, and data structures associated with the decryption process.

String analysis is another useful technique for identifying indicators of the decrypted payload within the memory or binary. Analysts can search for known strings or signatures that are characteristic of the payload's content, helping to pinpoint its location within memory or the binary.

Advanced decryption techniques may involve the development of custom scripts or tools to automate the decryption process. Analysts may write scripts that simulate the malware's execution and capture the decrypted payload as it is generated during runtime.

Emulation environments can also be employed to simulate the execution of the malware containing the encrypted payload. Emulators allow analysts to execute the malware and monitor its interactions with the emulated environment, facilitating the decryption process.

Static analysis techniques can provide insights into the encryption algorithm and decryption routine used by the malware. Analysts may disassemble the malware binary using tools like IDA Pro or Ghidra to analyze the code responsible for decryption.

Pattern recognition is a technique that involves identifying known encryption algorithms or patterns used by the malware. Analysts can create custom scripts or tools to recognize patterns in the binary's structure or behavior that indicate the presence of encryption routines.

Signature-based detection can be employed to identify known encryption algorithms or encryption keys used by the malware. Analysts can compare the binary's characteristics to a database of known encryption signatures to determine the encryption method used.

In some cases, decrypting encrypted payloads may require reverse engineering the encryption algorithm itself. Analysts must analyze the malware's decryption routine, reverse the encryption process, and develop custom decryption tools or scripts to recover the original content.

Dynamic debugging techniques can aid in decrypting encrypted payloads by allowing analysts to step through the decryption routine and monitor memory and register changes in real-time. Debuggers like OllyDbg or WinDbg can be used for this purpose.

Behavioral analysis can provide valuable insights into the decryption process. Analysts can observe how the malware interacts with the system and external resources during execution, helping to understand the decryption routine's behavior and identify key components.

Decrypting encrypted payloads is a complex and challenging task that often requires a combination of techniques and tools. Analysts must possess a deep understanding of encryption algorithms, assembly language, and the inner workings of the malware to successfully decrypt encrypted content.

Successful decryption of encrypted payloads is crucial in understanding the full capabilities and behavior of the malware, enabling analysts to develop effective countermeasures and protections against the threat.

Chapter 5: Evading Anti-Analysis and Obfuscation Techniques

Anti-analysis evasion strategies are tactics employed by malware authors to hinder the efforts of security researchers, analysts, and automated systems attempting to analyze and reverse-engineer malicious code. These strategies are designed to make the malware more resilient to analysis, protect its functionality, and evade detection by security solutions.

One common anti-analysis evasion strategy is the use of packers and crypters. Packers are programs that compress and encrypt the malware's code, making it difficult for analysts to understand and extract the original content. Crypters go a step further by encrypting the entire malware binary and providing a decryption routine at runtime, ensuring that the code remains hidden until executed.

Another anti-analysis technique involves the use of obfuscation. Obfuscation is the process of intentionally adding complexity to the code to make it harder to understand. This includes renaming variables, functions, and labels with meaningless or random names, as well as inserting dead code or junk instructions to confuse analysts.

Malware authors often employ anti-debugging techniques to thwart the efforts of analysts using debuggers to inspect and trace the code. Anti-debugging measures can include checks for debugging flags, such as the presence of a debugger, breakpoints, or tracing tools, and the use of techniques to terminate the malware when analysis tools are detected.

Timing-based evasion tactics involve introducing delays or timing checks within the malware's code. These checks may involve waiting for a specific period before executing malicious actions, making it challenging for analysts to capture the malware's behavior within a controlled environment.

Environment checks are anti-analysis techniques that involve inspecting the execution environment to determine whether the malware is running in a controlled analysis environment or a real user's system. If the malware detects the presence of analysis tools or sandboxes, it may alter its behavior or remain dormant to avoid detection.

Code encryption and decryption are techniques that involve encrypting parts of the malware's code or data and decrypting them at runtime. This makes it difficult for analysts to examine the code statically and requires them to trace the execution flow to understand the behavior of the malware.

Polymorphism and metamorphism are advanced anti-analysis strategies that involve dynamically changing the malware's code or structure with each infection or execution. Polymorphic malware generates different code variations for each infection, while metamorphic malware continuously modifies its code, making it challenging for signature-based detection and static analysis.

Anti-sandbox techniques are designed to detect and evade sandbox environments often used for analyzing malware. These techniques involve monitoring system calls, network activity, and environmental characteristics to identify sandbox behaviors. When detected, the malware may alter its behavior or remain dormant to avoid detection.

Rootkit functionality is employed by some malware to gain persistence and maintain control over an infected system. Rootkits operate at a low level within the operating system, making them difficult to detect and analyze. They can hide processes, files, and network connections, making it challenging for analysts to identify malicious activities.

Injection attacks are anti-analysis tactics used by malware to inject malicious code into legitimate processes or system components. This technique makes it difficult for analysts to trace the malware's behavior, as it appears to be part of a legitimate application or system service.

Self-modifying code is a technique in which the malware modifies its own code at runtime, making it challenging for analysts to predict the behavior of the malware or understand its actions through static analysis.

Packaging the malware with legitimate or trusted files is a technique used to disguise malicious code. By embedding malware within seemingly harmless files or documents, attackers can evade suspicion and make it harder for analysts to identify the malware's presence.

Fileless malware is an advanced anti-analysis strategy that operates entirely in memory without leaving traditional file traces on disk. This makes it difficult for traditional endpoint security solutions to detect and analyze fileless malware, as there are no files to scan or analyze.

Fileless malware is an advanced anti-analysis strategy that operates entirely in memory without leaving traditional file traces on disk. This makes it difficult for traditional endpoint security solutions to detect and analyze fileless malware, as there are no files to scan or analyze.

To counter these anti-analysis evasion strategies, analysts must employ advanced techniques and tools. This includes using custom scripts and automation to bypass anti-analysis checks, employing dynamic analysis environments that mimic real user systems, and developing behavioral analysis techniques to detect malicious behavior patterns even when traditional analysis methods fail.

In summary, anti-analysis evasion strategies are sophisticated techniques employed by malware authors to impede the efforts of security researchers and analysts. To effectively analyze and combat malware, analysts must stay ahead of these evasion tactics, continually adapt their methodologies, and employ a combination of static and dynamic analysis techniques, as well as behavioral analysis and advanced tools.

Dealing with obfuscated code is a fundamental challenge in the field of malware analysis and reverse engineering, as obfuscation techniques are commonly used by malware authors to conceal their code's functionality and thwart analysis efforts.

Obfuscation is the practice of intentionally adding complexity to code to make it harder to understand or reverse-engineer. Malware authors use obfuscation to protect their intellectual property, evade detection by security solutions, and make it challenging for analysts to uncover the malware's true behavior.

One prevalent form of obfuscation is code obfuscation, which involves renaming variables, functions, and labels with meaningless or random names. This makes it difficult for analysts to discern the purpose and functionality of different code elements, as the names no longer provide meaningful clues.

Control flow obfuscation is another obfuscation technique that alters the flow of program execution. This can involve adding unnecessary branches, loops, or jumps, making it challenging for analysts to follow the code's logic and understand its behavior.

String obfuscation is employed to hide sensitive strings, such as API function names, URLs, or encryption keys, within the code. Malware authors may use techniques like string encryption or encoding to obscure the strings, making them unreadable without proper decryption or decoding.

Data obfuscation involves manipulating data structures and formats to make it difficult for analysts to interpret the data's meaning and purpose. This can include encoding or encrypting data within the code, making it challenging to extract and analyze.

Mathematical obfuscation involves using complex mathematical operations or equations within the code to obfuscate its functionality. Analysts must decipher these equations to understand the code's behavior accurately.

Anti-analysis measures are often integrated with obfuscated code to detect the presence of analysis tools and evade detection. These measures can include checks for debugging flags, breakpoints, or tracing tools, as well as techniques to terminate the malware when analysis tools are detected.

Constant modification is a form of obfuscation where constants used within the code are frequently changed. This requires analysts to track the values of these constants during execution, adding complexity to the analysis process.

Dynamic code generation is an advanced obfuscation technique where the malware generates and executes code at runtime. This code may be entirely different from the original code, making it challenging for analysts to predict the malware's behavior.

To deal with obfuscated code effectively, analysts employ various techniques and tools to reverse-engineer and understand the code's functionality. One common approach is to use disassemblers and decompilers, such as IDA Pro or Ghidra, to generate human-readable code from the obfuscated binary.

Static analysis involves examining the code without executing it, and while obfuscation can make static analysis more challenging, it is still a valuable technique for understanding code structure and logic. Analysts can identify code patterns, control flow, and data flow to gain insights into the malware's behavior.

Dynamic analysis, on the other hand, involves executing the obfuscated code within a controlled environment and monitoring its behavior during runtime. Dynamic analysis allows analysts to observe the code's actions, interactions with the system, and any attempts to evade analysis.

Debuggers are essential tools in dealing with obfuscated code, as they enable analysts to step through the code, set breakpoints, and inspect memory and registers at critical points. This helps analysts understand the code's execution flow and behavior.

Memory analysis tools, such as Volatility or Rekall, can aid in dealing with obfuscated code by allowing analysts to examine the contents of the system's RAM during malware execution. Memory analysis can reveal important data structures, decrypted strings, and runtime behavior.

Pattern recognition is a valuable technique for identifying known obfuscation methods or patterns within the code. Analysts can create custom scripts or tools to recognize obfuscation signatures and apply appropriate deobfuscation techniques.

Decryption and deobfuscation scripts can be developed to automate the process of decrypting strings, decoding data, or reversing specific obfuscation techniques used by the malware. These scripts simplify the analysis process and enhance efficiency.

Obfuscation-aware debugging involves using debuggers that are specifically designed to handle obfuscated code. These debuggers can automatically recognize and deobfuscate code elements, making it easier for analysts to navigate and understand the code.

In summary, dealing with obfuscated code is a critical aspect of malware analysis and reverse engineering. While obfuscation can significantly complicate the analysis process, analysts have a range of techniques and tools at their disposal to overcome these challenges, ultimately enabling them to understand and combat malicious code effectively.

Chapter 6: Reverse Engineering Malware Communication Protocols

Analyzing malware network communication is a crucial aspect of malware analysis and cybersecurity, as it provides valuable insights into the behavior of malicious software and helps identify potential threats to an organization's network and data.

Malware often communicates with external servers or command and control (C2) infrastructure as part of its malicious activities, such as exfiltrating data, receiving commands, or downloading additional payloads. Analyzing this network traffic can reveal the malware's intentions, capabilities, and the extent of its impact on a compromised system.

One fundamental step in analyzing malware network communication is capturing and monitoring network traffic. Analysts can employ network sniffing tools, like Wireshark or tcpdump, to capture packets exchanged between the infected host and external servers. This captured data provides a detailed view of the malware's network activity.

Packet analysis involves inspecting the captured packets to extract relevant information, such as IP addresses, ports, protocols, and payload data. Analysts can use this data to identify communication patterns, understand the protocols used, and recognize potential indicators of compromise (IOCs).

Protocol analysis is essential for dissecting the communication protocols employed by the malware. Malware may use standard protocols like HTTP, DNS, or IRC to communicate, or it may use custom protocols specific to its operation. Analysts must decode and interpret these protocols to uncover the malware's actions.

Traffic analysis involves analyzing the frequency, volume, and timing of network communication events. Unusual traffic patterns, high data transfer rates, or spikes in communication may indicate malicious activity. Analysts look for anomalies that suggest data exfiltration, lateral movement, or C2 communication.

Payload analysis focuses on extracting and examining the data exchanged between the malware and external servers. This can include decrypted or encoded payloads, HTTP responses, and command messages. Analysts must decode and decrypt payloads to understand their content and purpose.

Domain and IP analysis is essential for identifying the servers and domains that the malware communicates with. Analysts can check these domains against threat intelligence feeds, reputation databases, and blacklists to assess their reputation and potential association with malicious activity.

Reverse DNS and WHOIS queries can provide additional information about the domains and IP addresses involved in the malware's network communication. This information may reveal the registrants or organizations behind the infrastructure.

GeoIP analysis helps analysts determine the geographic locations of IP addresses associated with the malware's network communication. Understanding the geographical distribution of malicious infrastructure can aid in threat attribution and mitigation.

Behavioral analysis of network communication involves assessing the malware's actions, such as data exfiltration, lateral movement, or command execution, based on the observed network traffic. Analysts must piece together the malware's behavior from the network evidence.

Pattern recognition is a valuable technique for identifying known malware communication patterns or IOCs within the network traffic. Analysts can create custom signatures or use threat intelligence feeds to detect malicious indicators.

Traffic correlation involves cross-referencing network communication with other indicators, such as host-based logs, system artifacts, or memory analysis results. Correlation can provide a more comprehensive view of the malware's impact on the system.

SSL/TLS inspection is crucial for analyzing encrypted network communication. Many malware samples use encryption to hide their activities. Analysts can use SSL/TLS inspection tools to decrypt and inspect encrypted traffic for malicious content.

Network decoys and honeypots are used to attract and analyze malicious network traffic. Decoys mimic vulnerable systems, while honeypots are dedicated environments designed to lure and monitor attackers. These setups can capture valuable information about malware behavior.

Real-time monitoring of network traffic is vital for identifying ongoing attacks or infections. Intrusion detection systems (IDS) and intrusion prevention systems (IPS) can help automate the detection and blocking of malicious network communication.

Automated malware sandboxes can execute malware samples in controlled environments while monitoring their network behavior. Sandboxes provide insights into how malware operates and communicates without exposing real systems to risk.

Post-analysis reporting is essential for documenting the findings of network communication analysis. Analysts should create comprehensive reports that detail the malware's behavior, communication patterns, IOCs, and any mitigation recommendations.

In summary, analyzing malware network communication is a critical skill for cybersecurity professionals and malware analysts. It provides essential insights into the behavior of malicious software and helps organizations defend against cyber threats. By employing various techniques and tools, analysts can dissect and understand the intricate network activities of malware, aiding in threat detection, mitigation, and response efforts.

Reverse engineering protocol patterns is an essential aspect of analyzing and understanding how software and systems communicate with each other over networks, whether for legitimate or malicious purposes.

Protocols are sets of rules and conventions that govern the format and sequence of data exchanged between different entities in a networked environment.

Analyzing protocol patterns involves dissecting the structure and behavior of these protocols to gain insights into how they function, the data they transmit, and the specific patterns they follow.

Reverse engineers, security analysts, and network experts often engage in protocol pattern analysis to uncover the inner workings of proprietary or undocumented protocols, as well as to identify and mitigate vulnerabilities or malicious activities.

Protocol analysis typically begins with the collection of network traffic or packet captures that contain the communication between systems or applications.

Packet captures are raw data recordings of network traffic that include details like source and destination addresses, port numbers, packet payloads, and protocol-specific information.

To effectively reverse engineer protocol patterns, analysts use specialized tools and techniques, such as packet sniffers or protocol analyzers, which allow them to inspect and interpret the captured network traffic.

One of the fundamental steps in protocol pattern analysis is identifying the protocol in use. This involves recognizing the unique characteristics and patterns within the captured traffic that correspond to a particular protocol.

Common indicators for identifying protocols include well-known port numbers, headers, initial handshakes, or specific data patterns that are characteristic of the protocol.

Once the protocol is identified, analysts proceed to dissect the protocol's structure, starting with the headers and data fields that make up each packet.

Understanding the header fields is crucial, as they often contain essential information, such as source and destination addresses, sequence numbers, flags, and checksums, which determine how the data is processed and interpreted.

By examining the header fields, analysts can identify key elements of the protocol, such as control messages, acknowledgment mechanisms, or error handling procedures.

Protocol analyzers and dissectors are valuable tools that assist in the extraction and interpretation of protocol headers and data fields.

These tools can automatically decode and display protocol-specific information, making it easier for analysts to comprehend the structure of the protocol.

Beyond headers, protocol patterns also encompass the sequences and behaviors exhibited by systems or applications following the protocol.

For example, some protocols may follow a strict request-response pattern, where one entity sends a request, and the other responds accordingly.

Analyzing these sequences helps in understanding the logic and flow of communication within the protocol.

Protocol state machines are often employed to represent the various states and transitions that entities go through during protocol communication.

Reverse engineers can create state machines to model the behavior of a protocol, helping them visualize the possible sequences and conditions that dictate the protocol's operation.

By mapping out these states and transitions, analysts gain a clearer picture of the protocol's inner workings.

Furthermore, protocol pattern analysis involves studying the data payloads exchanged within the protocol.

Data payloads can contain a wide range of information, from application-specific messages to actual user data.

Analyzing data payloads may require knowledge of data formats, encoding schemes, and data structures used by the protocol.

For instance, analyzing HTTP traffic involves understanding content types, status codes, and message formats like JSON or XML.

Additionally, encryption and compression techniques applied to data payloads must be considered during protocol pattern analysis.

Reverse engineers may need to decrypt or decompress data to access its original content.

Some protocols may use cryptographic mechanisms to secure data, requiring analysts to reverse engineer encryption algorithms or obtain encryption keys.

Analyzing protocol patterns also entails identifying any variations or deviations from standard protocol specifications.

Some proprietary or custom protocols may exhibit unique features or modifications that deviate from established standards.

Reverse engineers must carefully examine these variations to ensure accurate analysis and interpretation.

Furthermore, protocol pattern analysis often involves the creation of custom dissectors or parsers that can handle non-standard or proprietary protocols.

These dissectors help decode and display protocol-specific information within packet captures, aiding analysts in their reverse engineering efforts.

Pattern recognition plays a significant role in protocol pattern analysis. Analysts look for recurring patterns, sequences, or anomalies within the protocol traffic.

These patterns may be indicative of specific behaviors or operations within the protocol.

For example, a pattern that consistently appears before a data transfer may signal the initiation of a file transfer operation within a protocol.

By identifying and documenting these patterns, analysts can develop a comprehensive understanding of the protocol's functionality.

Reverse engineering protocol patterns also involves testing and validation of the analyzed patterns. Analysts often create test scenarios or use crafted packets to validate their understanding of the protocol's behavior.

Validation helps ensure the accuracy of the reverse engineering process and confirms that the protocol patterns are correctly interpreted.

Once the protocol patterns are thoroughly analyzed, documented, and validated, analysts can use this knowledge for various purposes.

In a security context, understanding protocol patterns can aid in identifying and mitigating vulnerabilities, as well as detecting malicious activities or intrusions.

Security analysts can develop detection signatures or rules based on known protocol patterns to monitor network traffic for suspicious or unauthorized behavior.

Moreover, protocol pattern analysis can be valuable for network troubleshooting and optimization.

By understanding how protocols function and interact, network administrators can diagnose and resolve performance issues, ensuring efficient and reliable communication.

In summary, reverse engineering protocol patterns is a multifaceted process that involves the collection, identification, dissection, and interpretation of network traffic to gain insights into the operation of protocols.

Security analysts, reverse engineers, and network experts use specialized tools, techniques, and pattern recognition to understand the behavior, structure, and data exchange within protocols.

This knowledge is essential for various purposes, including security analysis, network optimization, and protocol implementation or emulation.

Chapter 7: Advanced Code Reversing Strategies

Advanced techniques in code reversing encompass a range of sophisticated methods employed by reverse engineers and security analysts to dissect and understand complex software systems, applications, and malware.

Code reversing, also known as reverse engineering, involves the process of deconstructing software binaries or executables to reveal their underlying logic, functionality, and algorithms.

While basic code reversing techniques provide valuable insights, advanced techniques are necessary when dealing with intricate software or when the code is intentionally obfuscated to hinder analysis.

One advanced technique in code reversing involves dynamic analysis using debuggers and disassemblers. Debuggers allow analysts to step through the code execution, set breakpoints, and inspect the memory and register contents during runtime.

This real-time approach is especially useful for understanding the flow of the code and the interactions with the operating system and external libraries.

Disassemblers, on the other hand, convert the binary code into human-readable assembly language, enabling analysts to study the code's logic and structure in detail.

Another advanced technique is the use of memory forensics. Memory forensics involves examining the contents of a system's RAM (Random Access Memory) during the execution of a program or malware.

Analyzing memory dumps can reveal critical information, such as data structures, encryption keys, and runtime behaviors, which may not be apparent through static analysis alone.

Dynamic taint analysis is an advanced technique that tracks the flow of data within a program or malware. It allows analysts to identify the sources of input that influence specific program behaviors.

By tracing the tainted data, analysts can pinpoint vulnerabilities, potential attack vectors, or hidden functionality within the code.

Advanced code analysis tools and plugins are essential in code reversing. These tools automate and enhance the reverse engineering process by providing advanced analysis features, such as function identification, control flow graph generation, and data flow analysis.

One example of a powerful tool is Ghidra, an open-source software reverse engineering framework developed by the National Security Agency (NSA).

Another advanced technique is the utilization of symbolic execution and symbolic debugging. Symbolic execution allows analysts to explore different program paths and inputs symbolically, identifying potential vulnerabilities or paths that lead to specific outcomes.

Symbolic debugging tools assist in understanding complex code by providing symbolic representations of program states, variables, and expressions.

Advanced reverse engineers may employ techniques like dynamic binary instrumentation (DBI) or dynamic program analysis frameworks like Intel Pin or DynamoRIO.

DBI tools insert custom code into a program at runtime, enabling fine-grained monitoring and manipulation of program behavior. This is especially useful for tracing complex code execution and gathering runtime information.

In cases where proprietary or undocumented protocols are encountered, reverse engineers often resort to protocol reverse engineering. This advanced technique involves dissecting network protocols or data formats used by software to exchange information.

Reverse engineers analyze packet captures, reverse engineer protocol implementations, and create custom parsers to understand how data is structured and transmitted.

Malware analysis and reverse engineering often require advanced techniques due to the evolving sophistication of malicious code. One crucial aspect is sandbox evasion, where malware attempts to detect and evade analysis environments.

To counter these efforts, analysts may employ sandbox detection evasion techniques, such as environment simulation, to create analysis environments that mimic real user systems.

Another advanced malware analysis technique is code emulation, where the malware is executed within a controlled environment that emulates the target operating system and hardware.

This allows analysts to observe the malware's behavior without infecting real systems and provides insight into its functionality and capabilities.

Code deobfuscation is essential when dealing with obfuscated or encrypted code in malware samples. Reverse engineers use various deobfuscation techniques to transform the code into a more readable and understandable form.

This may involve deobfuscating control flow, decrypting strings or payloads, and reversing anti-analysis measures employed by the malware.

Advanced code reversing often necessitates the use of specialized tools and plugins designed for specific tasks. These tools can automate repetitive tasks, facilitate code analysis, and provide valuable insights into program behavior. Examples of such tools include IDA Pro, OllyDbg, Radare2, and Binary Ninja.

In summary, advanced techniques in code reversing are indispensable for comprehending complex software, malware, and proprietary protocols. These techniques encompass dynamic analysis, memory forensics, symbolic execution, protocol reverse engineering, and sandbox evasion countermeasures.

Reverse engineers employ a combination of tools, frameworks, and expertise to unravel intricate code, identify vulnerabilities, and gain insights into the inner workings of software and malware. Advanced code reversing skills are essential in the ever-evolving field of cybersecurity and software analysis. Strategies for dealing with polymorphic malware are crucial in the field of cybersecurity, as polymorphic malware presents a significant challenge to traditional security measures and requires specialized approaches to detection, analysis, and mitigation.

Polymorphic malware is a type of malicious software that constantly changes its appearance or code structure to evade detection by security solutions and analysts.

This constant transformation makes it difficult for signature-based antivirus programs to identify polymorphic malware, as traditional signatures become outdated quickly.

One effective strategy for dealing with polymorphic malware involves employing heuristic and behavioral analysis techniques. Heuristic analysis focuses on identifying suspicious or unusual behaviors exhibited by a program, rather than relying on known signatures.

By monitoring the behavior of an executable, security solutions can flag potential threats based on actions such as file modifications, registry changes, or network communication patterns.

Behavioral analysis takes heuristic analysis a step further by observing the program's actions in a controlled environment or sandbox. Sandboxing allows security analysts to observe the malware's behavior without exposing their own systems to risk.

During behavioral analysis, analysts can track system interactions, file accesses, and network communications to identify malicious behavior, even when the malware has polymorphic features.

Another strategy is to utilize machine learning and artificial intelligence (AI) algorithms for malware detection. Machine learning models can be trained on large datasets of known malware and benign samples, allowing them to identify patterns and anomalies in code and behavior.

These models can adapt to changes in malware techniques and may be effective at detecting polymorphic malware based on deviations from expected behavior.

Furthermore, employing signature-less intrusion detection systems (IDS) that rely on anomaly detection can be an effective approach. Anomaly-based IDS systems establish a baseline of normal system behavior and trigger alerts when deviations, such as those caused by polymorphic malware, are detected.

Regularly updating and patching software and systems can be a fundamental strategy to mitigate the risk of polymorphic malware infections. Vulnerabilities in software are often exploited by malware, and by keeping systems up to date, organizations can reduce potential entry points for malware.

Network segmentation is another valuable strategy for containing the spread of polymorphic malware within a network. Segmented networks isolate critical systems and limit lateral movement, making it harder for malware to propagate.

Intrusion prevention systems (IPS) can complement network segmentation by actively blocking suspicious or malicious traffic patterns. Polymorphic malware often exhibits unusual network behavior, which IPS systems can detect and prevent.

Another strategy is to implement application whitelisting, where only approved and trusted applications are allowed to run on endpoints and servers. This restricts the execution of unapproved code, making it difficult for polymorphic malware to infiltrate the system.

Continuous monitoring and threat hunting are essential strategies to identify polymorphic malware within an environment. Security teams should actively look for signs of compromise, unusual behavior, or anomalies that may indicate the presence of polymorphic malware.

Threat hunting involves proactively searching for threats by analyzing network and system logs, looking for indicators of compromise (IOCs), and using forensic techniques to identify potential security breaches.

Implementing security information and event management (SIEM) systems can aid in centralized log management and correlation of security events, helping organizations detect and respond to polymorphic malware incidents more efficiently.

Regularly educating and training employees on security best practices is a crucial strategy for reducing the risk of polymorphic malware infections. Social engineering attacks, often used to deliver polymorphic malware, can be mitigated through user awareness and vigilance.

Furthermore, endpoint detection and response (EDR) solutions can play a vital role in identifying and mitigating the effects of polymorphic malware. EDR tools provide visibility into endpoint activities, allowing security teams to respond quickly to suspicious behavior and contain malware outbreaks.

Maintaining a robust incident response plan is essential for effectively handling polymorphic malware incidents. Organizations should have clear procedures in place for containing, eradicating, and recovering from malware infections.

Regularly backing up critical data and systems can mitigate the impact of a polymorphic malware attack, as it allows for the restoration of affected systems to a clean state.

Collaboration with threat intelligence providers and information sharing within the cybersecurity community is another valuable strategy. Sharing threat intelligence on polymorphic malware variants and attack techniques can help organizations stay informed and better prepared to defend against evolving threats.

Finally, organizations should consider the use of specialized security tools and services designed to detect and mitigate polymorphic malware. These tools often incorporate advanced detection techniques, such as code emulation and behavioral analysis, to identify and respond to polymorphic threats effectively.

In summary, dealing with polymorphic malware requires a multi-faceted approach that combines advanced detection techniques, behavioral analysis, machine learning, network segmentation, intrusion prevention, threat hunting, user education, incident response planning, and collaboration with the broader cybersecurity community.

Polymorphic malware is a dynamic and evolving threat, and organizations must continuously adapt their strategies and defenses to effectively mitigate the risks associated with it.

Chapter 8: Memory Forensics and Malware Detection

Memory analysis tools and approaches play a critical role in the field of digital forensics and incident response, providing investigators with the means to extract valuable information from a computer's volatile memory.

Memory analysis is the process of examining the contents of a computer's RAM (Random Access Memory) to uncover evidence related to system activities, running processes, and potentially malicious actions.

One of the primary motivations for memory analysis is to identify and investigate security incidents, such as malware infections, unauthorized access, and data breaches.

Memory analysis can also be used in digital forensics to gather evidence for criminal investigations, uncovering activities like data theft, system compromise, or user actions.

Memory analysis tools come in various forms, ranging from standalone applications to integrated solutions within larger digital forensics frameworks.

One widely used memory analysis tool is Volatility, an open-source framework designed to extract information from memory dumps obtained from Windows, Linux, and macOS systems.

Volatility provides a wide range of plugins that allow investigators to examine running processes, network connections, loaded drivers, open files, and more.

Another popular memory analysis tool is Rekall, which is also open-source and highly extensible. Rekall supports multiple memory image formats and offers a flexible framework for creating custom analysis plugins.

The Sleuth Kit (TSK) is a collection of open-source command-line tools for forensic analysis, including memory analysis. TSK provides capabilities for examining memory dumps and identifying processes and objects.

Commercial solutions like Magnet AXIOM and Encase Forensic also offer memory analysis features as part of their comprehensive digital forensic suites.

Approaches to memory analysis can be broadly categorized into two categories: live analysis and offline analysis.

Live analysis involves examining a running system's memory while it is still operational. This approach is useful for real-time incident response and may help identify ongoing malicious activities.

However, live analysis may also introduce risks, as it can potentially alter the state of the system or tip off attackers if not conducted discreetly.

Offline analysis, on the other hand, involves analyzing memory dumps obtained from a system that has been shut down or suspended. This approach eliminates the risk of altering the system's state during analysis.

Memory dumps can be acquired through various methods, such as using dedicated tools like DumpIt, capturing crash dumps, or leveraging virtual machine snapshots.

When conducting memory analysis, investigators typically focus on several key areas:

Process and thread examination: Memory analysis tools can reveal information about running processes, their associated threads, and their memory usage. Investigators can identify suspicious or malicious processes and their memory footprints.

Network connections: Analyzing memory dumps can provide insights into network connections established by running processes. Investigators can identify communication with malicious IP addresses or domains.

Registry and file system artifacts: Memory analysis tools can extract information from a system's registry and file system, even if they are in use. This can reveal evidence of malware persistence mechanisms and file operations.

Artifacts related to user activity: Investigators can uncover user-related artifacts in memory, including user credentials, open files, and user activities, which may be crucial in digital forensics cases.

Malware indicators: Memory analysis can help identify indicators of compromise (IOCs) related to malware infections, such as memory-resident malicious code, injected threads, or suspicious processes.

Volatile data: Memory analysis allows for the retrieval of volatile data, such as clipboard contents, command history, and cached passwords, which can be valuable for investigations.

Rootkit and kernel-level analysis: Memory dumps enable investigators to scrutinize the kernel space, detecting rootkits and kernel-level modifications that may be associated with advanced malware.

Malicious behavior patterns: Memory analysis tools can identify patterns of malicious behavior, such as privilege escalation, code injection, or code execution in memory.

To enhance the effectiveness of memory analysis, investigators often employ memory forensics frameworks and community-developed knowledge bases. These resources provide guidance, best practices, and analysis techniques for specific memory analysis scenarios.

Furthermore, the application of artificial intelligence (AI) and machine learning (ML) to memory analysis is an emerging trend. AI and ML algorithms can assist in automating the detection of anomalies and potential threats in memory dumps, reducing the time and effort required for analysis.

In summary, memory analysis tools and approaches are indispensable in digital forensics and incident response, enabling investigators to extract vital information from volatile memory for the purpose of identifying security incidents, uncovering evidence, and conducting comprehensive forensic examinations.

These tools, whether open-source or commercial, offer a range of capabilities for examining processes, network connections, registry and file system artifacts, user activity, and malicious behavior patterns.

With the ever-evolving threat landscape, memory analysis continues to evolve, incorporating AI and ML techniques to improve the efficiency and accuracy of investigations, ultimately contributing to a more robust cybersecurity posture.

Detecting and analyzing malware in memory is a critical aspect of cybersecurity, as many sophisticated threats employ memory-resident techniques to evade traditional security measures.

Memory-resident malware, also known as fileless malware, operates solely within a computer's volatile memory (RAM), leaving no footprint on the hard drive.

This stealthy behavior makes memory-resident malware challenging to detect and analyze, necessitating specialized approaches and tools.

The primary motivation for detecting and analyzing memory-resident malware is to identify and mitigate threats that conventional antivirus solutions may miss.

Memory-resident malware can execute malicious code directly in RAM, exploit vulnerabilities, or manipulate legitimate processes to carry out malicious activities.

Detecting such malware requires a multifaceted approach that combines behavior-based analysis, memory forensics, and endpoint security measures.

Behavior-based analysis focuses on monitoring the behavior of running processes and identifying anomalous or suspicious activities.

This approach looks for signs of malicious code injection, privilege escalation, or unusual system interactions that may indicate the presence of memory-resident malware.

Memory forensics, on the other hand, involves the extraction and examination of memory dumps obtained from a compromised system.

Memory dumps capture the contents of a system's RAM at a specific point in time and serve as valuable sources of evidence for malware analysis.

To acquire memory dumps, investigators can use specialized tools, such as Volatility or Rekall, which allow them to capture the memory state of a live system or a suspended virtual machine.

Once acquired, memory dumps can be analyzed to identify memory-resident malware and gain insights into its behavior.

Memory analysis involves scrutinizing the memory dump to locate suspicious or malicious processes, code injection points, and artifacts left behind by the malware.

Researchers and analysts look for telltale signs of memory-resident malware, such as unallocated memory regions, hidden processes, or abnormal registry entries.

Furthermore, memory analysis can reveal the presence of rootkits or stealthy components that operate at a kernel level, making them difficult to detect through traditional means.

Endpoint security measures are essential for preventing memory-resident malware from infiltrating systems in the first place.

This includes implementing advanced endpoint protection solutions that can detect and block malicious activities in real time.

Additionally, maintaining up-to-date software and operating systems is crucial to patching known vulnerabilities that memory-resident malware might exploit.

Educating end users about the risks of phishing attacks and social engineering can also reduce the likelihood of malware infection.

Memory-resident malware often enters a system through malicious email attachments, compromised websites, or unpatched software.

For organizations, implementing network security measures such as intrusion detection systems (IDS) and intrusion prevention systems (IPS) can help identify and block suspicious network traffic associated with memory-resident malware.

These systems can detect communication patterns, command-and-control traffic, and other indicators of compromise.

Moreover, continuous monitoring and threat hunting are essential for identifying memory-resident malware within an organization's environment.

Security teams should actively search for signs of compromise, unusual process behaviors, or anomalous network traffic that may indicate the presence of malware.

Threat hunting involves examining logs, conducting memory analysis, and using forensic techniques to uncover and respond to potential security incidents.

Machine learning and artificial intelligence (AI) are increasingly being employed to improve the detection of memory-resident malware.

These technologies can analyze vast amounts of data, including memory dump content and network traffic patterns, to identify anomalies and potentially malicious behavior.

Machine learning models can be trained on labeled datasets of known malware and benign samples, allowing them to recognize patterns and deviations indicative of memory-resident malware.

Furthermore, security solutions that combine endpoint detection and response (EDR) with behavioral analysis can provide real-time insights into system activities and identify memory-resident threats.

Advanced EDR tools can flag suspicious processes, memory injections, or malicious behavior patterns for further investigation.

In summary, detecting and analyzing memory-resident malware requires a comprehensive approach that encompasses behavior-based analysis, memory forensics, endpoint security measures, network security controls, user education, and continuous monitoring.

Memory analysis tools like Volatility and Rekall play a crucial role in uncovering memory-resident malware, while machine learning and AI technologies enhance the efficiency of detection.

With the increasing sophistication of memory-resident malware, organizations and security professionals must remain vigilant, continuously adapting their strategies to mitigate the risks associated with these stealthy threats.

Chapter 9: Exploiting Vulnerabilities in Malware

Identifying and exploiting weaknesses in malware is a crucial aspect of cybersecurity and threat analysis, as it allows security professionals to gain insights into the inner workings of malicious code and develop effective countermeasures.

Malware, designed to compromise systems and steal data, often exhibits vulnerabilities or weaknesses that can be leveraged by security researchers, analysts, and incident responders.

The identification of these weaknesses involves a systematic process of analysis, reverse engineering, and experimentation.

One common weakness found in malware is the presence of coding errors or vulnerabilities that can be exploited by security experts.

These errors may include buffer overflows, integer overflows, use-after-free vulnerabilities, and more, which can lead to crashes or unexpected behavior when manipulated.

Identifying such coding errors requires a deep understanding of programming languages, assembly code, and binary analysis.

Exploiting these vulnerabilities can result in the termination of malicious processes or even the complete disruption of malware operations.

Another weakness in malware is the reliance on external resources or infrastructure for command-and-control (C2) communication.

Malware often needs to connect to a remote server or network to receive instructions, exfiltrate data, or download additional payloads.

Security analysts can monitor and intercept this network traffic to gain insights into the C2 infrastructure, identify malicious domains or IP addresses, and block or disrupt the communication channels.

Exploiting this weakness involves setting up monitoring systems, capturing network traffic, and potentially redirecting traffic to controlled systems to gather intelligence on the attacker's infrastructure.

Furthermore, some malware may contain hardcoded or plaintext credentials for authentication to C2 servers, databases, or other resources.

Identifying these credentials within the malware's code can provide security professionals with access to the attacker's infrastructure, allowing them to monitor or disrupt malicious activities.

Exploiting this weakness may involve connecting to the attacker's infrastructure, monitoring their activities, and collecting valuable intelligence for attribution or remediation.

Malware may also rely on specific vulnerabilities or exploits to compromise systems or escalate privileges.

Identifying these vulnerabilities can lead to the development of patches or mitigations to protect systems from exploitation.

Exploiting these weaknesses in malware can involve conducting vulnerability assessments, penetration testing, or applying patches to vulnerable systems to prevent further infections.

Additionally, malware often employs evasion techniques to avoid detection by security solutions.

These techniques may include polymorphism, obfuscation, or encryption to make the malware's code appear different each time it runs.

Identifying weaknesses in these evasion techniques can involve reverse engineering and code analysis to develop signatures or heuristics that can detect malware despite its attempts to evade detection.

Exploiting these weaknesses may involve creating detection rules or improving the capabilities of security solutions to identify and block polymorphic or obfuscated malware.

Another weakness found in some malware is the lack of proper error handling or exception handling mechanisms.

When malware encounters unexpected situations or errors, it may crash or behave unpredictably.

Identifying these weaknesses can involve analyzing the malware's code for error-handling routines and identifying potential vulnerabilities.

Exploiting this weakness may result in the malware crashing or failing to execute as intended, disrupting its malicious activities.

Furthermore, malware often relies on specific environmental conditions or configurations to operate effectively.

Identifying these dependencies can help security professionals devise strategies to disrupt or neutralize malware.

Exploiting this weakness may involve altering system configurations, creating honeypot environments, or manipulating the malware's perception of its environment to hinder its functionality.

Additionally, some malware strains have vulnerabilities or weaknesses that can be targeted by security researchers to gain control over the infected system.

Identifying these weaknesses may involve in-depth analysis and experimentation to understand the malware's behavior and vulnerabilities.

Exploiting these weaknesses can result in the removal of the malware or the recovery of compromised systems.

In summary, identifying and exploiting weaknesses in malware is a crucial aspect of cybersecurity and threat analysis.

Security professionals use a combination of reverse engineering, code analysis, network monitoring, vulnerability assessments, and experimentation to uncover vulnerabilities, errors, or dependencies within malware.

Exploiting these weaknesses can lead to the disruption of malicious operations, the development of effective countermeasures, and the protection of systems and data from cyber threats.

Case studies of vulnerability exploitation provide valuable insights into the real-world impact of security vulnerabilities and the importance of effective vulnerability management practices.

Vulnerabilities, whether in software, hardware, or systems, represent weaknesses that can be exploited by attackers to compromise the security and integrity of an organization's assets.

In this section, we will explore several case studies that illustrate the consequences of unpatched vulnerabilities and the exploitation of security flaws.

The Equifax data breach, one of the most notable cybersecurity incidents in recent history, serves as a prime example of the severe consequences of unpatched vulnerabilities.

In 2017, Equifax, a major credit reporting agency, fell victim to a data breach that exposed the personal and financial information of approximately 147 million individuals.

The breach occurred due to the exploitation of a known vulnerability in the Apache Struts web application framework.

Despite a patch being available for the vulnerability, Equifax failed to apply it in a timely manner, leaving their systems exposed to attackers.

The consequences of this oversight were significant, resulting in massive financial losses, reputational damage, and legal repercussions for the company.

Another case study involves the WannaCry ransomware attack that swept across the globe in 2017.

WannaCry exploited a vulnerability in the Microsoft Windows operating system, known as EternalBlue, which had been patched by Microsoft prior to the attack.

However, many organizations had not applied the necessary security updates, leaving them vulnerable to the ransomware.

The attack affected critical infrastructure, healthcare institutions, and businesses worldwide, causing widespread disruption and financial losses.

The NotPetya ransomware attack, which targeted Ukrainian organizations in 2017, is another case study that highlights the devastating impact of vulnerability exploitation.

NotPetya initially spread through a compromised software update for a tax accounting application widely used in Ukraine.

Once inside a network, the malware used multiple vulnerabilities and lateral movement techniques to propagate and encrypt data.

NotPetya caused extensive damage, disrupting operations and data access for numerous organizations, including large multinational corporations.

The attack had significant financial implications and raised awareness about the importance of securing software supply chains.

A notable case study involving a hardware vulnerability is the Spectre and Meltdown vulnerabilities discovered in modern microprocessors in 2018.

These vulnerabilities allowed attackers to potentially access sensitive data by exploiting speculative execution in CPUs.

The discovery of Spectre and Meltdown prompted a rush to develop and distribute patches and firmware updates to mitigate the risks.

However, the complexity of the vulnerabilities and the need for coordinated efforts across the tech industry made the response challenging.

These case studies underscore the critical role that vulnerability management plays in cybersecurity.

Organizations must have robust processes in place for identifying, prioritizing, and patching vulnerabilities promptly.

Failure to do so can result in severe financial losses, reputational damage, and legal liabilities.

Effective vulnerability management also involves the coordination of security teams, the implementation of patch management solutions, and the monitoring of systems for emerging threats.

Furthermore, the case studies emphasize the importance of regular security awareness training for employees.

Many breaches and vulnerabilities are exploited through social engineering techniques, such as phishing emails, which can be mitigated through user education and awareness.

In addition to these case studies, it is crucial to consider the role of responsible disclosure and collaboration within the cybersecurity community.

Ethical hackers and security researchers often discover vulnerabilities in software and systems.

Responsible disclosure allows them to report these vulnerabilities to the affected organizations so that patches can be developed and deployed before malicious actors can exploit them.

Collaboration between security researchers, vendors, and organizations helps improve overall cybersecurity by identifying and addressing vulnerabilities before they are weaponized.

In summary, case studies of vulnerability exploitation provide valuable lessons for the cybersecurity community.

They underscore the importance of timely patching, vulnerability management, security awareness, and responsible disclosure in mitigating the risks associated with security vulnerabilities.

The consequences of unpatched vulnerabilities can be severe, resulting in data breaches, financial losses, and damage to an organization's reputation.

By learning from these case studies and implementing robust cybersecurity practices, organizations can better protect their assets and reduce their exposure to cyber threats.

Chapter 10: Case Studies and Expert-Level Malware Analysis

In-depth analysis of complex malware samples is a critical task in the field of cybersecurity, requiring skilled researchers and specialized tools to unravel the intricacies of malicious code and understand its full scope.

Complex malware, often designed with sophistication and evasion in mind, poses significant threats to organizations and individuals, making comprehensive analysis essential.

The goal of in-depth analysis is not only to identify and mitigate the immediate threat posed by the malware but also to uncover its underlying mechanisms, origins, and potential connections to threat actors.

Complex malware often employs multiple layers of obfuscation and evasion techniques to avoid detection by traditional security measures.

These techniques can include code obfuscation, encryption, polymorphism, and anti-analysis mechanisms, which make it challenging to analyze and dissect the malware.

To begin the analysis process, researchers typically obtain a copy of the malware sample, either through a controlled environment or from an infected system.

They then isolate the sample to prevent any potential harm or unintended consequences, ensuring that the analysis environment is fully controlled and isolated from the network.

Static analysis is one of the initial steps in the analysis of complex malware samples.

This involves examining the malware's code without executing it, allowing researchers to identify key characteristics, such as file headers, strings, functions, and libraries.

Static analysis can reveal clues about the malware's purpose, capabilities, and potential targets.

Dynamic analysis, on the other hand, involves executing the malware within a controlled environment, such as a sandbox or virtual machine, to observe its behavior.

During dynamic analysis, researchers monitor the malware's interactions with the system, file operations, network communication, and any attempts to evade detection or analysis.

By analyzing the malware's behavior in real-time, researchers can gain insights into its functionality and potential impact.

Reversing the malware's code is a critical aspect of in-depth analysis, involving the conversion of machine code into human-readable code, such as assembly language or higher-level programming languages.

This step allows researchers to understand the malware's logic, algorithms, and data structures, aiding in the identification of malicious functionalities.

Reverse engineering also reveals how the malware communicates with command and control servers, retrieves additional payloads, and carries out malicious activities.

During the analysis process, researchers often encounter anti-analysis techniques designed to thwart their efforts.

These may include checks for debugging environments, sandboxes, or virtual machines, as well as the use of code encryption or decryption routines.

Researchers must employ various techniques to bypass or neutralize these anti-analysis measures, allowing them to continue their analysis unhindered.

Memory analysis is another crucial component of in-depth analysis, as some malware operates primarily in a system's volatile memory, leaving no traces on disk.

Memory analysis tools like Volatility enable researchers to extract valuable information from memory dumps, such as running processes, network connections, and injected code.

This reveals the malware's runtime behavior, providing insights that may not be obtainable through traditional static or dynamic analysis.

Furthermore, researchers may conduct network analysis to trace the malware's communication with remote servers and understand its command and control infrastructure.

This involves capturing network traffic, analyzing protocols, and identifying patterns that can help uncover the malware's origins and objectives.

In-depth analysis of complex malware often requires collaboration between security researchers, incident responders, and threat intelligence teams.

Sharing findings, indicators of compromise (IOCs), and threat intelligence helps enhance the community's understanding of emerging threats and aids in the development of countermeasures.

After completing the analysis, researchers document their findings, producing detailed reports that include information about the malware's characteristics, behavior, indicators, and potential mitigation strategies.

These reports are invaluable for incident response, threat intelligence, and developing defensive measures to protect against similar threats in the future.

In summary, in-depth analysis of complex malware samples is a multifaceted process that demands expertise, specialized tools, and a structured approach.

Researchers employ static and dynamic analysis, reverse engineering, memory analysis, and network analysis to uncover the malware's inner workings, behaviors, and objectives.

This knowledge is crucial for developing effective countermeasures, enhancing cybersecurity, and mitigating the risks posed by sophisticated malware threats.

Collaboration and information sharing within the cybersecurity community are essential to staying ahead of evolving threats and protecting against complex malware attacks.

Expert-level insights gleaned from real-world case studies provide a unique perspective into the intricate world of cybersecurity and the ever-evolving landscape of cyber threats.

These case studies offer valuable lessons, best practices, and strategic approaches that can help organizations and security professionals bolster their defenses and respond effectively to cyber incidents.

One notable case study involves the Stuxnet worm, a highly sophisticated piece of malware that targeted Iran's nuclear facilities in the late 2000s.

Stuxnet demonstrated an unprecedented level of complexity and sophistication, employing multiple zero-day vulnerabilities to infect air-gapped systems and manipulate industrial control systems (ICS).

The Stuxnet case underscores the importance of air-gapped systems and the potential risks posed by state-sponsored cyberattacks on critical infrastructure.

It also highlights the necessity of proactive threat intelligence and the need for international cooperation to address cyber threats that transcend borders.

Another illuminating case study revolves around the NotPetya ransomware attack, which affected organizations worldwide in 2017.

Initially disguised as ransomware, NotPetya was designed to cause widespread disruption and destruction rather than generate ransom payments.

The malware used a compromised software update to spread rapidly across networks, encrypting data and rendering systems inoperable.

NotPetya's impact extended beyond financial losses, as it disrupted global supply chains and raised awareness about the vulnerability of software supply chains.

The case underscores the importance of software supply chain security, patch management, and the need for robust incident response plans.

Furthermore, the case of the Sony Pictures breach in 2014 provides insights into the consequences of a cyberattack on an entertainment company.

The breach involved the theft of sensitive data, including unreleased films, confidential emails, and employee information, followed by the exposure of this data by the attackers.

The case illustrates the risks of insider threats, the importance of data protection, and the need for comprehensive cybersecurity measures, including user training and awareness.

Additionally, the Mirai botnet case study sheds light on the evolving landscape of Internet of Things (IoT) threats.

Mirai targeted insecure IoT devices, recruiting them into a botnet that was used to launch distributed denial of service (DDoS) attacks.

The case underscores the significance of securing IoT devices, the implications of insecure defaults, and the growing threat posed by botnets in the IoT era.

Furthermore, the case of the SolarWinds supply chain attack in 2020 provides a sobering reminder of the challenges posed by advanced persistent threats (APTs).

The attackers compromised a trusted software vendor, infiltrating their software updates to distribute a backdoor to thousands of organizations.

This sophisticated attack demonstrated the need for supply chain security, threat hunting, and the importance of continuous monitoring for anomalous behavior.

The case also emphasized the role of incident response in containing and mitigating APT attacks.

A more recent case study involves the Colonial Pipeline ransomware attack in 2021, which disrupted fuel supplies in the United States.

The attack highlighted the vulnerabilities of critical infrastructure to cyber threats and the potential cascading effects on daily life.

It underscored the importance of proactive cybersecurity measures, incident response planning, and collaboration with law enforcement agencies.

Moreover, the case study of the REvil ransomware gang's activities offers insights into the ransomware-as-a-service (RaaS) model.

REvil operated a highly profitable RaaS operation, targeting high-profile victims and demanding hefty ransoms.

This case illustrates the sophistication of ransomware operations, the need for strong data backup and recovery practices, and the importance of international law enforcement efforts against cybercriminals.

These case studies collectively provide expert-level insights into the multifaceted challenges of modern cybersecurity.

They emphasize the significance of threat intelligence, proactive defense measures, supply chain security, incident response, and collaboration within the cybersecurity community.

While each case study represents a unique set of circumstances, they all underscore the need for organizations and security professionals to stay vigilant, adapt to evolving threats, and prioritize cybersecurity as an integral part of their operations.

By drawing from the lessons learned in these real-world cases, organizations can strengthen their cybersecurity posture and better protect their assets, data, and reputation in an increasingly digital world.

BOOK 3
MALWARE ANALYSIS AND REVERSE ENGINEERING
A COMPREHENSIVE JOURNEY

ROB BOTWRIGHT

Chapter 1: Introduction to Malware Analysis and Reverse Engineering

The importance of malware analysis in the field of cybersecurity cannot be overstated, as it plays a pivotal role in defending against and mitigating the ever-evolving threat landscape.

Malware, short for malicious software, encompasses a broad range of malicious code, including viruses, worms, Trojans, ransomware, spyware, and more, all designed with harmful intent.

Understanding the significance of malware analysis begins with recognizing the pervasive and dynamic nature of cyber threats that organizations and individuals face daily.

Malware is a primary weapon in the arsenal of cybercriminals and nation-state actors, enabling them to compromise systems, steal sensitive data, disrupt operations, and perpetrate fraud.

One of the fundamental reasons why malware analysis is crucial is its role in identifying and characterizing new and emerging threats.

Malware is constantly evolving, with attackers developing new tactics, techniques, and evasion methods to bypass traditional security measures.

By dissecting and analyzing malware samples, security professionals can gain insights into the latest attack vectors, vulnerabilities, and trends, allowing them to adapt their defenses accordingly.

Additionally, malware analysis aids in the development of detection signatures and security measures that can be used to identify and block known threats.

This proactive approach is vital for protecting systems and networks from malware that has already been discovered and documented.

Moreover, malware analysis helps organizations identify indicators of compromise (IOCs), such as file hashes, network traffic patterns, and behavior patterns, which can be used to detect and respond to ongoing or potential attacks.

The timely detection and containment of malware infections can significantly reduce the impact and damage caused by cyberattacks.

Malware analysis is also indispensable in incident response and forensic investigations.

When a security breach occurs, it is essential to determine the extent of the compromise, trace the attacker's activities, and identify the vulnerabilities or weaknesses that were exploited.

Malware analysis can provide critical insights into the attack timeline, the goals of the attacker, and the potential data breaches or data exfiltration that may have occurred.

Furthermore, malware analysis contributes to the development of effective mitigation and remediation strategies.

Security professionals can use the information gathered from malware analysis to close vulnerabilities, patch systems, and implement security controls that prevent future infections or attacks.

Another aspect of the importance of malware analysis is its role in attribution, which involves identifying the threat actors or groups responsible for specific malware campaigns.

Attribution is a complex process that often relies on a combination of technical analysis, geopolitical context, and threat intelligence.

By tracing the infrastructure, tactics, and tools used by attackers, researchers can build a profile of the threat actor and their motivations.

This information can be invaluable for law enforcement agencies, policymakers, and organizations seeking to defend against or respond to cyber threats.

Furthermore, malware analysis extends to studying advanced persistent threats (APTs), which are sophisticated, long-term cyber espionage campaigns conducted by well-resourced threat actors.

Understanding APTs and their tactics requires in-depth analysis of malware used in these campaigns, as APTs often employ custom-built, highly targeted malicious software.

By dissecting APT malware, security experts can uncover the full scope of an adversary's capabilities and intentions, aiding in the development of countermeasures and proactive defense strategies.

Additionally, malware analysis is instrumental in the development of threat intelligence, which involves collecting, analyzing, and disseminating information about emerging threats and vulnerabilities.

This intelligence can be shared across organizations and security communities to enhance collective defense efforts.

Furthermore, malware analysis is essential for ensuring the security of critical infrastructure, such as power grids, transportation systems, and healthcare facilities.

The potential consequences of malware attacks on these systems are far-reaching, impacting public safety and national security.

Analyzing malware that targets critical infrastructure helps identify vulnerabilities and weaknesses that could be exploited by malicious actors.

In summary, the importance of malware analysis in the realm of cybersecurity cannot be overstated.

It serves as a cornerstone for identifying, understanding, and mitigating the diverse and evolving threats that organizations and individuals face.

Malware analysis plays a crucial role in threat detection, incident response, attribution, defense strategy development, and the protection of critical infrastructure.

As the cyber threat landscape continues to evolve, the need for skilled malware analysts and robust analysis techniques remains paramount in safeguarding digital ecosystems and data from malicious actors.

The reverse engineering process is a crucial discipline within the field of cybersecurity, enabling security professionals to dissect and understand software, hardware, or systems in intricate detail.

This process involves the systematic deconstruction of a product, application, or device to reveal its internal workings, architecture, and design.

Reverse engineering serves various purposes, including the identification of vulnerabilities, the extraction of proprietary information, and the enhancement of interoperability with third-party software.

To embark on the reverse engineering journey, professionals must possess a combination of technical skills, critical thinking, and a deep understanding of computer systems.

The first step in the reverse engineering process typically involves acquiring a copy of the target software, hardware, or system.

This can be obtained legally through legitimate channels or, in some cases, through forensic analysis of a compromised system.

Once the target is in hand, the reverse engineer begins the analysis by studying the binary code or structure of the software or system.

This often involves examining the binary executable files, libraries, or firmware that make up the target.

Static analysis techniques play a pivotal role in the initial phase of reverse engineering.

Static analysis entails examining the code and data structures without executing the program, allowing the reverse engineer to identify key components, functions, and data.

By understanding the structure of the software or system, the reverse engineer gains insights into its functionality and potential vulnerabilities.

Next, dynamic analysis comes into play, involving the execution of the target software or system within a controlled environment.

Dynamic analysis allows the reverse engineer to observe the program's behavior, interactions with the operating system, and external communications.

During dynamic analysis, the reverse engineer can identify runtime vulnerabilities, memory-related issues, and unintended consequences of the program's execution.

Debugging tools and techniques are essential for dynamic analysis, as they enable the reverse engineer to step through the code, set breakpoints, and inspect the program's state in real-time.

Reverse engineers often employ disassemblers and decompilers to convert machine code into human-readable assembly language or higher-level programming languages.

This transformation makes it easier to analyze the program's logic, algorithms, and control flow.

Additionally, decompilation can reveal high-level language constructs, making it possible to understand the software's functionality and design more comprehensively.

As the reverse engineering process unfolds, the reverse engineer may encounter anti-reverse engineering techniques employed by the software or system's creators.

These measures can include code obfuscation, encryption, or integrity checks designed to thwart analysis.

Overcoming these obstacles requires creativity, perseverance, and a deep understanding of reverse engineering techniques.

In the case of software, the reverse engineer may also encounter binary protection mechanisms, such as software guards or anti-debugging routines.

These mechanisms aim to detect or hinder the use of reverse engineering tools, requiring the reverse engineer to employ evasion techniques or specialized tools to circumvent them.

In hardware reverse engineering, professionals often work with physical devices, such as integrated circuits (ICs) or printed circuit boards (PCBs).

Hardware reverse engineering can involve techniques such as decapping ICs to expose the silicon die, imaging PCBs for circuit analysis, or extracting firmware from embedded devices.

Understanding the hardware's schematics, connections, and logic is critical for comprehending its functionality and potential vulnerabilities.

Furthermore, reverse engineering can be instrumental in uncovering security flaws, vulnerabilities, or undocumented features within software, hardware, or systems.

By identifying and analyzing these weaknesses, security professionals can help organizations address and mitigate potential risks.

In some cases, reverse engineering can reveal vulnerabilities that could be exploited by malicious actors, necessitating prompt remediation.

Reverse engineering also plays a pivotal role in the realm of cybersecurity research and threat intelligence.

Security researchers use reverse engineering techniques to analyze malware, exploits, and cyberattacks, contributing to the development of threat intelligence and the creation of effective defenses.

Additionally, reverse engineering contributes to the discovery of zero-day vulnerabilities, which are previously unknown vulnerabilities that can be exploited by attackers.

When security researchers uncover these vulnerabilities, they can work with vendors to develop patches and protect users from potential threats.

In summary, the reverse engineering process is a multifaceted and essential discipline within the field of cybersecurity.

It involves the systematic analysis of software, hardware, or systems to understand their internal workings, vulnerabilities, and design.

Reverse engineering encompasses static and dynamic analysis, the use of disassemblers and decompilers, and the overcoming of anti-reverse engineering techniques.

The insights gained from reverse engineering are invaluable for identifying vulnerabilities, enhancing security, and contributing to cybersecurity research and threat intelligence.

As cyber threats continue to evolve, the role of reverse engineering remains indispensable in defending against emerging risks and safeguarding digital ecosystems.

Chapter 2: Setting Up Your Malware Analysis Environment

Selecting the appropriate tools and software is a critical decision for individuals and organizations involved in various fields, from information technology to cybersecurity.

The choice of tools can significantly impact productivity, efficiency, and the ability to achieve specific objectives.

Before delving into the selection process, it's essential to clarify the purpose and requirements for which the tools and software will be used.

This entails understanding the specific tasks, goals, and challenges that need to be addressed, whether it's network monitoring, data analysis, or malware detection.

Additionally, it's crucial to consider factors such as budget constraints, compatibility with existing systems, and the skill level of users who will operate the tools.

In many cases, the first step in choosing the right tools and software involves conducting a thorough needs assessment.

This involves gathering input from relevant stakeholders to determine their requirements and preferences.

Stakeholders may include IT professionals, security experts, data analysts, or other individuals who will use the tools in their day-to-day work.

Once the needs assessment is complete, the next step is to research and evaluate available options in the market.

This can be a daunting task, as there are often numerous tools and software solutions that claim to address similar needs.

To streamline the selection process, it's helpful to create a list of essential features and functionalities required for the tasks at hand.

For example, if the goal is to choose a network monitoring tool, the list may include features like real-time traffic analysis, alerting capabilities, and support for multiple platforms.

Moreover, it's important to consider the scalability of the tools and whether they can grow with the organization's needs over time.

Additionally, organizations should evaluate the reputation and credibility of the software vendors or tool providers.

This can be accomplished by researching customer reviews, seeking recommendations from trusted sources, and examining case studies or success stories related to the products.

It's also advisable to consider the vendor's track record in terms of updates, support, and commitment to security.

The security of the tools and software being evaluated is a paramount concern, especially in the context of cybersecurity.

Vulnerabilities or weaknesses in software can introduce significant risks to an organization's digital infrastructure.

Thus, it's crucial to assess the security features of the tools and whether they adhere to industry standards and best practices.

This includes considering aspects like data encryption, access controls, and vulnerability management.

Compatibility with existing systems and infrastructure is another vital aspect of the selection process.

The tools and software should seamlessly integrate with the organization's current technology stack to avoid disruptions and streamline operations.

Moreover, organizations should assess the ease of implementation and the availability of technical support or documentation provided by the tool vendors.

Cost considerations play a substantial role in selecting the right tools and software.

Organizations must determine their budget constraints and evaluate the total cost of ownership (TCO) of the tools over the long term.

This includes not only the initial purchase cost but also ongoing expenses such as maintenance, licensing, and training.

Open-source solutions may be an attractive option for those with limited budgets, as they often provide cost-effective alternatives to commercial software.

However, it's essential to weigh the pros and cons of open source, including the availability of community support and the potential need for in-house expertise.

User-friendliness and usability are significant factors, as tools and software should be accessible and practical for the individuals who will use them.

Intuitive interfaces, comprehensive documentation, and user training options can contribute to a smoother adoption process.

To make an informed decision, organizations may opt to conduct proof-of-concept (PoC) trials or pilot implementations.

These trials allow users to test the tools and software in a real-world context and assess their suitability for the intended tasks.

Feedback from users during the PoC phase can provide valuable insights and help refine the selection process.

It's also essential to consider the long-term sustainability and vendor support for the chosen tools and software.

Organizations should evaluate whether the vendor has a roadmap for future development, including updates, patches, and feature enhancements.

Vendor lock-in should be avoided whenever possible, as it can limit flexibility and hinder the ability to adapt to changing needs.

When selecting tools and software, organizations should also take data privacy and compliance requirements into account.

Certain industries and regions have specific regulations governing the handling and protection of sensitive data.

Ensuring that the chosen tools and software align with these regulations is essential to avoid legal and financial consequences.

Finally, organizations should be prepared to revisit their tool and software choices periodically.

Technology evolves rapidly, and the tools that were ideal at one point may no longer meet the organization's needs in the future.

Regular assessments and updates to the toolset can help ensure that an organization remains competitive, secure, and efficient in an ever-changing digital landscape.

In summary, choosing the right tools and software is a critical process that requires careful consideration, research, and evaluation.

Organizations must define their needs, assess available options, prioritize features, consider compatibility, security, and cost, and involve relevant stakeholders in the decision-making process.

By following a structured and informed approach to tool and software selection, organizations can enhance their capabilities, streamline operations, and stay ahead in their respective fields.

Configuring a secure analysis environment is a crucial step in ensuring the safety and effectiveness of activities such as malware analysis, penetration testing, and digital forensics.

This controlled environment is designed to isolate potentially harmful code or activities from the rest of the network and systems.

Creating a secure analysis environment begins with defining the specific objectives and requirements of the analysis or testing process.

Whether it's dissecting malware, assessing vulnerabilities, or conducting digital forensics, a clear understanding of the goals is essential.

Once the objectives are established, it's time to select the appropriate hardware and software components for the analysis environment.

This may include dedicated hardware, virtual machines, or containers that can be isolated from the production network.

Security professionals often employ virtualization technologies to create isolated environments that can be easily configured, cloned, and reset as needed.

Isolation is a cornerstone of a secure analysis environment, as it prevents any unintended consequences or malicious code from impacting the broader network.

Segmenting the analysis environment from the production network helps contain potential threats and limits their reach.

Network isolation can be achieved through the use of virtual LANs (VLANs), firewalls, or dedicated physical networks.

Network traffic monitoring and logging are critical aspects of configuring a secure analysis environment.

By capturing and analyzing network traffic, security professionals can gain insights into the behavior of the analyzed software or systems.

Additionally, logging helps track any suspicious or unexpected activities during the analysis process.

Implementing strict access controls is another essential element of a secure analysis environment.

Access should be limited to authorized personnel who have undergone training and understand the risks and responsibilities associated with their tasks.

Multi-factor authentication (MFA) and strong password policies help protect against unauthorized access.

Physical security measures, such as locked server rooms or cabinets, can further enhance the security of the analysis environment.

To protect the integrity of the analysis environment, regular backups and snapshots should be performed.

In the event of unexpected issues, data corruption, or a security incident, backups ensure that the environment can be restored to a known good state.

Security updates and patch management are crucial for maintaining the integrity of the analysis environment.

Keeping the operating systems, applications, and security tools up-to-date helps prevent known vulnerabilities from being exploited during analysis.

However, it's essential to test updates thoroughly in a controlled environment to ensure they do not introduce unintended consequences.

A strict "no internet access" policy is often enforced in a secure analysis environment to minimize the risk of threats from the outside.

This isolation ensures that the environment remains self-contained and less susceptible to external attacks or interference.

In cases where internet access is required for analysis, a dedicated and heavily monitored connection may be established to limit exposure.

The use of security tools and monitoring solutions within the analysis environment is paramount.

Intrusion detection systems (IDS), intrusion prevention systems (IPS), and antivirus solutions can help identify and mitigate threats during analysis.

Additionally, endpoint protection measures, such as sandboxing, can be employed to safely execute potentially malicious code without risking the integrity of the environment.

Continuous monitoring of the analysis environment is essential to detect and respond to any suspicious activities or anomalies.

Security professionals should actively monitor logs, network traffic, and system behavior to identify any signs of compromise.

Regular audits and assessments can help ensure that the security controls and configurations within the analysis environment remain effective over time.

Collaboration and knowledge sharing among security professionals and analysts are key components of a secure analysis environment.

By sharing insights, techniques, and threat intelligence, the security community can collectively enhance the effectiveness of their analysis and response efforts.

Additionally, documentation and standard operating procedures (SOPs) play a vital role in ensuring consistency and repeatability within the analysis environment.

Documentation should cover all aspects of configuration, processes, and incident response procedures.

Education and training for personnel working within the analysis environment are fundamental.

Security professionals should stay up-to-date with the latest threats, techniques, and tools relevant to their analysis tasks.

Furthermore, security awareness training ensures that personnel are aware of security best practices and potential risks.

In summary, configuring a secure analysis environment is a critical endeavor in the field of cybersecurity.

It involves careful planning, hardware and software selection, network isolation, access controls, monitoring, and continuous improvement.

A well-configured analysis environment provides security professionals with a controlled and safe space to conduct activities like malware analysis, penetration testing, and digital forensics.

By adhering to security best practices and maintaining vigilance, organizations can enhance their capabilities to detect and respond to evolving cyber threats.

Chapter 3: Basic Concepts of Assembly Language

Assembly language is a low-level programming language that is closely tied to the architecture of a computer's central processing unit (CPU).

In assembly language, programs are written using mnemonics and symbols that correspond to the CPU's instruction set.

Unlike high-level programming languages, which use more human-readable syntax and abstract away many details of the hardware, assembly language provides a direct representation of the CPU's operations.

This direct relationship between assembly language and the CPU makes it a powerful tool for tasks that require precise control over hardware resources.

Assembly language is often used for tasks such as writing device drivers, operating system kernels, and embedded systems programming.

While assembly language can be more challenging to learn and use compared to high-level languages like Python or C++, it offers a level of control and optimization that is difficult to achieve with higher-level languages.

In this chapter, we will explore the fundamental concepts of assembly language programming, starting with an overview of the CPU architecture and instruction set.

The CPU, or central processing unit, is the "brain" of a computer, responsible for executing instructions and performing calculations.

Each CPU has its own unique instruction set, which defines the set of operations it can perform and the format of instructions.

The instructions in an assembly language program are typically written using a combination of mnemonics, registers, and memory operands.

Registers are small, fast storage locations within the CPU that can be used for temporary data storage and manipulation.

Memory operands refer to data stored in the computer's memory, which can be accessed and manipulated by the CPU.

Assembly language instructions can perform a wide range of operations, including arithmetic calculations, data movement, branching (conditional and unconditional), and input/output operations.

To illustrate these concepts, let's consider a simple assembly language program that adds two numbers together and stores the result in a memory location.

In assembly language, the program might look something like this:

sqlCopy code

MOV AX, 5 ; Load the value 5 into register AX MOV BX, 7 ; Load the value 7 into register BX ADD AX, BX ; Add the values in registers AX and BX MOV [result], AX ; Store the result in memory location 'result'

In this example, the program begins by loading the values 5 and 7 into registers AX and BX, respectively.

The **MOV** (move) instruction is used to copy data between registers and memory.

Next, the **ADD** instruction is used to add the values in registers AX and BX, storing the result in register AX.

Finally, the **MOV** instruction is used again to store the result in a memory location labeled 'result'.

This simple program demonstrates the basic structure of assembly language programs, which consist of a sequence of instructions that manipulate data in registers and memory.

Assembly language also allows for conditional branching, which enables programs to make decisions and execute different code paths based on conditions.

For example, an assembly language program might use a conditional branch instruction to jump to different parts of the code based on whether a certain condition is met.

Conditional branching is a fundamental concept in programming and is used extensively in assembly language to implement control flow.

Another important aspect of assembly language programming is understanding how data is represented and manipulated.

Data types in assembly language are typically limited to integers, and various sizes of integers (e.g., 8-bit, 16-bit, 32-bit) are commonly used.

Data can be stored in registers or memory, and different instructions are used to perform operations on data, such as addition, subtraction, multiplication, and division.

In addition to arithmetic operations, assembly language instructions can also perform bitwise operations, such as AND, OR, and XOR, which are used to manipulate individual bits within data.

Understanding data representation and manipulation is essential for writing efficient and correct assembly language programs.

Assembly language programming also requires a strong understanding of the CPU's architecture and instruction set.

Each CPU architecture has its own set of instructions and addressing modes, which determine how instructions access and manipulate data.

For example, the x86 architecture, which is used in many personal computers, has a rich instruction set with a wide range of operations.

In contrast, simpler architectures, such as those used in embedded systems or microcontrollers, may have a more limited instruction set.

To write assembly language programs for a specific CPU architecture, programmers must refer to the CPU's documentation and reference manuals, which provide detailed information about instruction formats, addressing modes, and other architectural details.

In summary, assembly language is a low-level programming language that provides direct control over a computer's hardware.

Assembly language programs consist of a sequence of instructions that manipulate data in registers and memory, perform arithmetic and bitwise operations, and implement control flow using conditional branching.

To become proficient in assembly language programming, one must have a solid understanding of the CPU's architecture and instruction set, as well as the ability to work with data in various formats and sizes.

In the following chapters, we will delve deeper into the intricacies of assembly language programming, covering topics such as instruction formats, addressing modes, and practical examples of assembly language code.

Understanding assembly language instructions is a fundamental aspect of programming in this low-level language.

Each assembly language instruction corresponds to a specific operation that the CPU can perform.

These instructions are written using mnemonics and operands that specify the details of the operation.

Mnemonics are symbolic representations of operations, making the code more human-readable.

Operands provide the necessary data for the instruction to operate on.

In assembly language, instructions typically consist of an operation mnemonic followed by one or more operands.

Operands can be registers, memory addresses, constants, or labels.

Registers are small, fast storage locations within the CPU, and they play a central role in assembly language programming.

Different CPU architectures have varying numbers and types of registers, each with specific purposes.

For example, the x86 architecture commonly used in personal computers has general-purpose registers like AX, BX, CX, and DX.

Registers are used to store and manipulate data during program execution.

Memory addresses represent locations in the computer's memory where data is stored.

Instructions can access and manipulate data stored in memory by specifying memory addresses as operands.

Constants are values that are directly specified in the instruction, like immediate values.

Labels are used as references to memory locations, typically in branch instructions or when working with data structures.

Assembly language instructions perform a wide range of operations, including data movement, arithmetic calculations, logical operations, and control flow.

Data movement instructions copy data from one location to another, such as between registers or between memory and registers.

For example, the MOV (move) instruction is used to transfer data.

Arithmetic instructions perform mathematical operations on data, including addition, subtraction, multiplication, and division.

Logical instructions perform bitwise operations, such as AND, OR, and XOR, which manipulate individual bits within data.

Control flow instructions enable programs to make decisions and change the flow of execution.

They include conditional branches, unconditional jumps, and subroutine calls and returns.

Conditional branches allow programs to execute different code paths based on conditions.

For instance, the JZ (jump if zero) instruction jumps to a different location in the code if a specified condition is met.

Unconditional jumps, like JMP (jump), transfer program control to a designated location without any conditions.

Subroutine instructions, such as CALL and RET, enable the organization of code into reusable modules.

These instructions allow a program to call a subroutine, execute it, and return to the original location.

Assembly language instructions are encoded in binary, with each mnemonic and operand represented by specific bit patterns.

The instruction encoding is architecture-specific and defined by the CPU's instruction set.

Assembly language programmers need to be familiar with the encoding details to write and understand assembly code effectively.

It's important to note that different CPU architectures have distinct assembly languages, and the same mnemonic may have different meanings or behaviors in different architectures.

For example, the MOV instruction in x86 assembly may perform a different operation from the MOV instruction in ARM assembly.

Additionally, addressing modes determine how operands are specified and accessed in instructions.

Common addressing modes include immediate, register, direct, indirect, and indexed.

The immediate addressing mode specifies a constant value directly as an operand.

The register addressing mode uses a register as an operand.

Direct addressing mode specifies a memory location directly as an operand.

Indirect addressing mode uses a memory location pointed to by a register or memory address as an operand.

Indexed addressing mode combines a base address with an offset specified by an index register to access memory.

Understanding addressing modes is essential for effective use of assembly language instructions.

It's worth noting that assembly language instructions often have side effects on flags or condition codes.

Flags are status bits that reflect the outcome of previous instructions, such as whether a result is zero, negative, or overflowed.

Many instructions in assembly language affect these flags, and they are often used in conditional branches and decision-making.

For example, after an arithmetic operation, the zero flag may be set if the result is zero, allowing subsequent conditional branches to make decisions based on this flag.

Assembly language programmers need to be aware of the flags affected by each instruction to ensure correct program behavior.

In summary, assembly language instructions are the building blocks of low-level programming.

They represent specific operations that the CPU can perform, using mnemonics and operands.

Operands can be registers, memory addresses, constants, or labels.

Instructions cover data movement, arithmetic, logical operations, and control flow.

Understanding the encoding, addressing modes, and flags associated with instructions is essential for effective assembly language programming.

In the chapters that follow, we will delve deeper into these concepts and provide practical examples of assembly language instructions in action.

Chapter 4: Static Analysis Techniques

File analysis and metadata examination are critical processes in the field of digital forensics and cybersecurity.

These activities involve the inspection and investigation of files and their associated metadata to extract valuable information and uncover potential security threats.

In digital forensics, file analysis is an essential step in the examination of electronic evidence for legal investigations.

Metadata, often referred to as "data about data," provides important details about a file, such as its creation date, modification history, author, and more.

By analyzing this metadata, digital forensic examiners can piece together a timeline of events and gain insights into a suspect's actions.

File analysis begins with the identification of the files to be examined, which could include documents, images, videos, databases, or any other digital artifacts.

The goal is to determine the nature and purpose of these files within the context of an investigation.

One of the primary objectives of file analysis is to extract relevant information from files without altering their content or metadata.

This process requires specialized tools and techniques to ensure the preservation of evidence and maintain the integrity of the original files.

One common technique in file analysis is known as file carving, which involves extracting data fragments from files or disk images, even if the file system has been damaged or deleted.

File carving tools search for file signatures and structures within raw data to reconstruct files and recover valuable information.

Another important aspect of file analysis is the examination of file headers and footers.

File headers contain metadata and information about the file's format, while footers often mark the end of a file.

Analyzing these components can reveal hidden or malicious content within files.

Metadata examination is a crucial component of file analysis, providing valuable insights into the history and attributes of a file.

Metadata can include information such as the file's size, creation date, modification date, access permissions, owner, and more.

In digital forensics, metadata examination can help determine when a file was created, accessed, or modified, potentially corroborating or refuting alibis in criminal cases.

Additionally, examining metadata can reveal the source of a file, such as the device or application used to create it, which can be valuable in tracking down the origins of evidence.

Metadata can also expose potential privacy concerns, as it may reveal sensitive information about individuals or organizations.

For example, examining the metadata of a document may uncover the author's name, the company they work for, or even their location.

This information can be crucial in investigations involving intellectual property theft, corporate espionage, or data breaches.

Metadata can also play a significant role in cybersecurity, as it can help identify indicators of compromise (IOCs) and detect suspicious activities.

For example, examining the metadata of a suspicious email attachment may reveal information about its source or purpose, aiding in the identification of phishing attempts or malware delivery.

Furthermore, metadata analysis can be used to track the movement of files within a network, helping security professionals identify potential data exfiltration or unauthorized access.

Metadata examination can be performed manually or using specialized tools and software.

These tools often provide features for extracting, parsing, and presenting metadata in a human-readable format, making it easier for analysts to interpret the information.

In addition to metadata examination, file analysis can involve the inspection of file contents, including the extraction of embedded objects, hidden data, and steganography.

Embedded objects are additional files or data concealed within other files.

For example, a document may contain embedded images, audio files, or macros that can be extracted and analyzed.

Hidden data refers to information that is not readily visible within a file but can be uncovered through various techniques, such as file structure analysis or hex editing.

Steganography involves the concealment of data within other data, such as hiding messages within image files.

File analysis can reveal the presence of hidden data or steganographic techniques, helping investigators uncover covert communications or malicious activities.

It's essential to note that file analysis and metadata examination should be conducted in a forensically sound manner, ensuring that evidence is admissible in legal proceedings.

This requires strict adherence to forensic protocols, such as maintaining chain of custody, documenting procedures, and preserving original files and metadata.

In summary, file analysis and metadata examination are critical processes in digital forensics and cybersecurity.

They involve the inspection and investigation of files and their associated metadata to extract valuable information, uncover potential security threats, and support legal investigations.

These activities play a crucial role in uncovering evidence, tracking digital activities, and enhancing the security of computer systems and networks.

Strings analysis and pattern recognition are indispensable tools in the fields of cybersecurity, digital forensics, and malware analysis.

In the realm of computer security, strings analysis refers to the process of identifying and extracting human-readable text or character sequences from binary files or memory dumps.

Strings, in this context, are sequences of characters or bytes that may include plain text, code snippets, configuration data, or any other form of readable information embedded within binary data.

Pattern recognition, on the other hand, involves identifying specific patterns or signatures within strings to uncover meaningful information or detect known threats.

Both strings analysis and pattern recognition are crucial for understanding the content and behavior of files, identifying potential security risks, and aiding in the investigation of cyber incidents.

Strings analysis can reveal valuable insights into the nature of binary files, helping analysts determine their purpose and functionality.

When analyzing malware, strings analysis can unveil clues about the malware's capabilities, intentions, and potential targets.

For example, malware often contains strings that correspond to command and control (C2) server addresses, encryption keys, or malicious URLs.

Identifying these strings can provide critical intelligence for blocking or mitigating threats.

Strings analysis can also expose hardcoded credentials, filenames, registry keys, or other sensitive information that may be exploited by an attacker.

In digital forensics, strings analysis plays a pivotal role in uncovering evidence related to criminal activities or data breaches.

Examining strings within memory dumps or disk images can reveal communication logs, chat transcripts, email content, or traces of malicious activity.

By extracting and analyzing these strings, investigators can piece together a timeline of events and gain insights into the actions of suspects.

Pattern recognition complements strings analysis by allowing analysts to identify specific sequences or structures within strings that are indicative of known threats or vulnerabilities.

For example, antivirus software often employs signature-based detection, where predefined patterns or signatures of known malware are used to identify malicious files or strings.

These signatures are created based on the unique character sequences or byte patterns that are commonly associated with a particular malware variant.

When a file or string matches a known signature, it is flagged as potentially malicious.

Pattern recognition techniques can also be used to detect malicious or suspicious behavior within network traffic.

Intrusion detection systems (IDS) and intrusion prevention systems (IPS) employ pattern recognition to identify abnormal network patterns or known attack patterns.

By recognizing patterns associated with common attacks, such as SQL injection or cross-site scripting (XSS), these systems can take action to block or alert on potentially malicious activities.

In addition to identifying threats, pattern recognition can aid in the recovery of valuable data.

For instance, when recovering files from a damaged storage device, file carving tools use predefined file structure patterns to reassemble fragmented files and extract usable data.

Pattern recognition is not limited to predefined signatures; it also encompasses the creation of custom patterns tailored to specific investigations.

Analysts can define patterns of interest based on their knowledge of the case, such as specific keywords, IP addresses, or regular expressions.

These custom patterns help narrow down the focus of the analysis and may reveal relevant information that would otherwise remain hidden.

To conduct strings analysis and pattern recognition effectively, analysts employ a variety of tools and techniques.

Strings analysis often begins with the use of simple command-line utilities like the "strings" tool on Unix-based systems, which extracts ASCII strings from binary files.

More advanced tools offer additional features, such as the ability to analyze non-ASCII character sets, extract Unicode strings, and decode encoded or encrypted data.

Pattern recognition, on the other hand, can involve the development of regular expressions or custom scripts to search for specific patterns within strings or network traffic.

Specialized software, such as regular expression testers and pattern matching libraries, are commonly used to refine and test patterns.

Machine learning techniques have also made significant strides in pattern recognition, allowing automated systems to learn and identify patterns in large datasets.

In cybersecurity, machine learning models can analyze network traffic or strings of code to detect anomalies or malicious patterns.

While strings analysis and pattern recognition are powerful tools, they are not without challenges.

Malware authors often employ techniques to obfuscate strings, such as encrypting or encoding them to evade detection.

Pattern recognition may also generate false positives when generic patterns match innocuous content.

Furthermore, the sheer volume of data and the dynamic nature of cyber threats make it essential for analysts to continuously update and refine patterns to stay effective.

In summary, strings analysis and pattern recognition are essential techniques in the fields of cybersecurity, digital forensics, and malware analysis.

They enable analysts to extract meaningful information from binary data, detect known threats, and uncover evidence of malicious activities.

By combining strings analysis and pattern recognition with other investigative techniques, professionals can enhance their ability to identify and respond to cyber threats effectively.

Chapter 5: Dynamic Analysis and Debugging

Setting up dynamic analysis environments is a crucial step in the field of malware analysis and cybersecurity.

Dynamic analysis involves the execution of suspicious or unknown software in a controlled environment to observe its behavior and assess its potential threats.

Creating an effective dynamic analysis environment requires careful planning, specialized tools, and adherence to best practices.

The first consideration when setting up a dynamic analysis environment is selecting the appropriate hardware and software.

A dedicated machine or virtual environment is typically used to isolate the analysis process from the analyst's host system.

Using virtualization technology, such as VMware or VirtualBox, allows for the creation of isolated sandboxes where malware can be executed safely.

These virtual machines (VMs) can be configured with different operating systems and software versions to match the diversity of potential malware targets.

The choice of the operating system is crucial, as different malware may target specific platforms, such as Windows, Linux, or macOS.

To maximize the effectiveness of the analysis environment, it's essential to keep the operating system and software up to date with security patches.

Additionally, the environment should be configured with minimal software to reduce potential attack surfaces and minimize interference with the analysis process.

Once the hardware and software are in place, the next step is to establish network connectivity within the analysis environment.

This connectivity allows the malware sample under analysis to communicate with the outside world, providing insight into its network behavior.

However, to prevent potential threats, network isolation and segmentation are critical.

Creating a separate network or subnet for the analysis environment ensures that any malicious activity is contained and does not affect other systems on the network.

Network traffic monitoring tools, such as Wireshark or tcpdump, should be installed to capture and analyze network communications during dynamic analysis.

Another essential aspect of setting up a dynamic analysis environment is the selection of monitoring and analysis tools.

These tools are used to observe the behavior of the malware as it runs within the controlled environment.

Dynamic analysis tools include debugger software, system monitoring utilities, and sandboxing solutions.

A debugger allows analysts to step through the execution of a program, inspect memory, and analyze the runtime behavior of the malware.

Popular debuggers include OllyDbg, IDA Pro, and WinDbg for Windows malware analysis.

For Linux malware analysis, GDB (GNU Debugger) is a commonly used tool.

In addition to debuggers, analysts should deploy system monitoring utilities to capture system-level events and changes caused by the malware.

These utilities can log file system modifications, registry changes, process creation and termination, network connections, and more.

Tools like Sysinternals Suite for Windows or auditd for Linux are valuable resources for this purpose.

Sandboxing solutions play a significant role in dynamic analysis by providing a controlled environment where malware can be executed safely.

Sandboxing tools create an isolated environment that mimics a real operating system, allowing the malware to run while capturing its behavior.

Popular sandboxing solutions include Cuckoo Sandbox, Joe Sandbox, and Hybrid Analysis.

Sandbox reports provide valuable insights into the malware's actions, such as file system modifications, network communications, and system calls.

To ensure the effectiveness of the dynamic analysis environment, it's essential to keep the sandboxing software up to date with the latest malware analysis capabilities and evasion techniques.

Another critical consideration is the proper configuration of security policies within the analysis environment.

Security policies define what actions are permitted and restricted during the analysis process.

By configuring policies to restrict certain actions, such as outbound network connections or file system modifications, analysts can control the malware's behavior and prevent it from causing harm.

However, it's essential to strike a balance between security and realism in the analysis environment.

Overly restrictive policies may lead to inaccurate results, as malware may behave differently when it encounters obstacles not present in real-world scenarios.

Moreover, analysts should consider implementing additional security measures, such as firewalls, intrusion detection systems (IDS), and antivirus software, to further protect the analysis environment.

In some cases, malware samples may attempt to evade analysis by detecting the presence of security tools or sandboxes.

To counter such evasion techniques, analysts can employ countermeasures, such as altering the environment's appearance to make it appear more like a typical user system.

These modifications can include changing system names, disguising the presence of monitoring tools, or manipulating system configurations.

Another aspect of dynamic analysis is the use of deception techniques, often referred to as "honey pots" or "honey tokens."

These are enticing artifacts placed within the environment to lure malware into revealing its capabilities and intentions.

Honey pots can include fake documents, network shares, or user accounts that appear valuable to malware.

By monitoring interactions with these deceptive elements, analysts can gain valuable insights into the malware's objectives.

A crucial aspect of setting up a dynamic analysis environment is documentation and record-keeping.

Analysts should maintain detailed records of the analysis process, including the initial setup, sample information, configuration changes, and observed behavior.

These records serve as a valuable resource for sharing findings with colleagues, reporting to management, or providing evidence in legal cases.

Finally, continuous improvement is essential for an effective dynamic analysis environment.

Analysts should regularly update tools, review and refine security policies, and stay informed about emerging threats and evasion techniques.

By evolving the analysis environment in response to evolving threats, analysts can maintain the highest level of efficacy in malware analysis and cybersecurity.

In summary, setting up dynamic analysis environments is a critical process in the fields of malware analysis and cybersecurity.

It involves selecting the appropriate hardware and software, configuring network connectivity, and deploying monitoring and analysis tools.

Security policies, evasion countermeasures, and documentation are essential elements of an effective analysis environment.

Continuous improvement and adaptation to emerging threats ensure the environment remains effective in identifying and mitigating security risks.

Debugging techniques are a fundamental aspect of malware analysis, enabling analysts to gain insights into a malware sample's behavior and functionality.

Debugging is the process of examining and manipulating a program's execution in a controlled environment to understand its inner workings.

In the context of malware analysis, debugging serves several critical purposes, such as uncovering malicious code, identifying evasion techniques, and extracting valuable intelligence.

There are various debugging techniques and tools available to analysts, each with its own strengths and applications.

One common debugging approach is using a debugger, a specialized software tool that allows analysts to control the execution of a program, inspect its memory, and examine its behavior step by step.

Popular debuggers like OllyDbg, WinDbg, and GDB (GNU Debugger) provide a user-friendly interface for interacting with a malware sample.

By attaching a debugger to a running process or opening a malware file within the debugger, analysts can halt execution at specific points, set breakpoints, and examine registers and memory content.

Breakpoints are a crucial feature of debugging, allowing analysts to stop execution at specific addresses, functions, or conditions.

When a breakpoint is hit, the debugger pauses the program's execution, enabling analysts to inspect the program's state and memory contents at that moment.

Breakpoints can be set on function calls, memory access, specific instructions, or any other event of interest.

In the context of malware analysis, breakpoints are often placed at the entry point of the malware's code or on functions suspected to be of importance.

Stepping through code is another essential debugging technique.

Analysts can execute the program one instruction at a time, allowing them to closely observe the malware's behavior and trace its execution path.

By stepping through code, analysts can monitor changes to registers and memory, inspect variables, and identify the malware's logic and functionality.

Conditional breakpoints are a powerful feature of debuggers, enabling analysts to break execution only when specific conditions are met.

For example, a conditional breakpoint can be set to break when a particular registry key is accessed or when a specific API function is called.

This allows analysts to focus their debugging efforts on critical areas of interest within the malware's code.

Another valuable debugging technique is the use of watchpoints, which are breakpoints triggered by changes to specific memory locations.

Watchpoints are especially useful for tracking modifications to critical data structures or variables.

When a watchpoint is hit, the debugger pauses execution and provides information about the change, allowing analysts to understand how the malware manipulates data.

In addition to traditional debuggers, some malware analysts use kernel-mode debuggers like WinDbg for Windows or kernel debugging in Linux.

Kernel debugging allows analysts to inspect and manipulate the behavior of the operating system and kernel-level code, providing deeper insights into malware's interactions with the system.

However, kernel debugging requires specific configurations and expertise, as it involves debugging the core of the operating system.

Another essential debugging technique is dynamic analysis, where analysts monitor the malware's runtime behavior without attaching a debugger directly.

Dynamic analysis often involves running the malware in a controlled environment, such as a sandbox or virtual machine, and capturing its behavior, including file system modifications, network communications, and process interactions.

Dynamic analysis tools, such as Process Monitor, Wireshark, and CaptureBAT, are commonly used to monitor and record system events during malware execution.

By combining dynamic analysis with debugging techniques, analysts can gain a comprehensive understanding of the malware's actions and intentions.

It's worth noting that malware often employs anti-analysis techniques to thwart debugging efforts.

Common anti-analysis techniques include code obfuscation, packing, and the use of anti-debugging tricks.

Code obfuscation involves the transformation of code to make it harder to understand, with techniques such as renaming variables, adding unnecessary instructions, and encrypting critical code sections.

Packers and crypters are tools used to compress and encrypt malware, making it more challenging for analysts to analyze and detect.

Anti-debugging tricks can include checks for the presence of a debugger, attempts to modify or erase debug-related memory, or evasion of specific debugging events.

To overcome these anti-analysis measures, malware analysts must employ various debugging tricks and techniques themselves.

For example, analysts can use kernel-level debuggers to debug user-mode malware, making it harder for the malware to detect debugging attempts.

Another strategy is using debugger plugins and scripts to automate repetitive tasks and streamline the analysis process.

These scripts can help analysts identify and neutralize anti-debugging measures, decrypt or deobfuscate code, and extract critical information.

In summary, debugging techniques are invaluable tools in malware analysis, allowing analysts to gain insights into a malware sample's behavior, identify evasion techniques, and extract valuable intelligence.

Debuggers, breakpoints, conditional breakpoints, and watchpoints provide analysts with fine-grained control over program execution.

Dynamic analysis complements debugging by enabling the monitoring of malware's runtime behavior without direct debugger attachment.

However, analysts must be prepared to overcome anti-analysis measures commonly employed by malware authors, using creative debugging tricks and techniques.

By mastering these debugging techniques, malware analysts can effectively dissect and understand the behavior of malicious software, contributing to improved cybersecurity and threat mitigation efforts.

Chapter 6: Code Deobfuscation and Anti-Analysis Techniques

Dealing with code obfuscation is a crucial aspect of malware analysis and reverse engineering.

Obfuscation is the deliberate act of making code more difficult to understand or reverse engineer.

Malware authors use code obfuscation techniques to protect their malicious software from analysis, detection, and attribution.

Understanding and overcoming code obfuscation is essential for malware analysts and cybersecurity professionals.

Code obfuscation can take various forms, such as renaming variables and functions with meaningless names, adding unnecessary code, and using encryption to hide critical parts of the code.

One common obfuscation technique is string obfuscation, where text strings within the code, such as URLs or API function names, are encrypted or encoded to prevent easy identification.

String obfuscation makes it challenging to determine the malware's functionality and communication patterns.

Another obfuscation technique is control flow obfuscation, where the order of instructions is altered, and conditional statements are added to confuse the program's logic.

Control flow obfuscation makes it difficult to discern the malware's execution flow and behavior.

Code splitting is a form of obfuscation that involves breaking a program into smaller, separate functions or modules that are harder to analyze individually.

These functions may be loaded dynamically at runtime, making it challenging to reconstruct the full program's logic.

Other obfuscation techniques include junk code insertion, where irrelevant or meaningless instructions are added to the code to confuse analysts, and arithmetic obfuscation, where mathematical operations are used to obfuscate numeric values and constants.

To deal with code obfuscation effectively, analysts must employ various reverse engineering techniques and tools.

One fundamental approach is code deobfuscation, which involves reversing the obfuscation transformations to reveal the original, unobfuscated code.

Deobfuscation can be a time-consuming and complex task, as it requires understanding the obfuscation techniques used and devising countermeasures.

Static analysis is a technique that involves examining the code without executing it, focusing on identifying patterns, logic, and data structures.

During static analysis, analysts can use disassemblers and decompilers to transform machine code into a more human-readable format, making it easier to analyze and understand.

Dynamic analysis, on the other hand, involves running the malware in a controlled environment and monitoring its behavior.

While dynamic analysis doesn't directly address code obfuscation, it can provide insights into the malware's actions and intentions, which can aid in understanding the obfuscated code.

One useful approach to dealing with code obfuscation is using automated deobfuscation tools and scripts.

These tools are designed to reverse common obfuscation techniques and simplify the analysis process.

For example, there are tools that can automatically decrypt or decode obfuscated strings within the code, making it easier to identify malicious URLs or commands.

Furthermore, some tools can help in detecting and removing unnecessary or redundant code added during obfuscation.

While automated tools can be valuable, they are not always sufficient, as sophisticated malware may employ custom obfuscation techniques that require manual intervention.

Manual analysis and reverse engineering expertise are often necessary to unravel complex code obfuscation.

One effective strategy is to focus on identifying key code patterns and critical functionality within the obfuscated code.

By understanding the malware's core functionality, analysts can prioritize their efforts and target specific areas for deobfuscation.

Additionally, experienced analysts can recognize obfuscation patterns and tricks commonly used by malware authors, making it easier to reverse engineer the code.

Collaboration among malware analysts and researchers can also be a valuable approach to dealing with code obfuscation.

Sharing insights, strategies, and tools for deobfuscation can lead to more effective analysis and a faster understanding of the malware's behavior.

Moreover, the cybersecurity community often collaborates to identify and document new obfuscation techniques and trends, enabling analysts to stay informed and adapt their approaches accordingly.

When dealing with code obfuscation, it's essential to exercise caution and use isolated, controlled environments for analysis to prevent accidental execution of potentially harmful code.

Furthermore, analysts should maintain detailed records of their analysis efforts, documenting their findings and the steps taken to reverse engineer obfuscated code.

These records can serve as a valuable resource for knowledge sharing and future reference.

In summary, dealing with code obfuscation is a fundamental aspect of malware analysis and reverse engineering.

Malware authors use obfuscation techniques to protect their code from analysis, making it challenging for cybersecurity professionals to understand and mitigate threats.

To overcome code obfuscation, analysts employ reverse engineering techniques, both manual and automated, and collaborate with peers to share insights and strategies.

By mastering the art of code deobfuscation and continuously adapting to evolving obfuscation techniques, cybersecurity professionals can enhance their ability to combat malware effectively and protect digital systems and networks.

Overcoming anti-analysis measures is a critical aspect of malware analysis and reverse engineering.

Malware authors employ various tactics and techniques to detect, evade, and hinder the analysis of their malicious software.

These anti-analysis measures are designed to make it more challenging for cybersecurity professionals and researchers to dissect and understand the malware's behavior and functionality.

To effectively overcome anti-analysis measures, analysts must employ a combination of technical expertise, creative problem-solving, and a deep understanding of the malware's evasion techniques.

One common anti-analysis measure used by malware authors is the detection of virtualized or sandboxed environments.

Malware may check for the presence of virtualization software or specific system attributes associated with sandboxes.

To overcome this, analysts can use techniques like "sandbox evasion" or "sandbox detection bypass" to make the malware believe it is running in a real, non-virtualized environment.

This can involve altering system attributes, registry keys, or environment variables to mimic a genuine system.

Another anti-analysis technique is the use of code obfuscation and packing, making it challenging for analysts to reverse engineer the malware.

Code obfuscation involves techniques like renaming variables, adding unnecessary instructions, and encrypting critical parts of the code.

Packing involves compressing and encrypting the malware, requiring decryption and unpacking before analysis.

To overcome these measures, analysts must employ code deobfuscation and unpacking techniques to restore the original, unobfuscated code.

This often requires in-depth knowledge of the obfuscation or packing methods used and the development of custom tools or scripts.

Malware may also employ anti-debugging tricks to thwart analysis.

These tricks can include checks for the presence of a debugger, attempts to modify or erase debug-related memory, or evasion of specific debugging events.

Analysts can use debugger plugins, scripts, or kernel-level debugging to counter these anti-debugging measures and gain control over the malware's execution.

Additionally, analysts must be prepared to identify and neutralize anti-analysis measures designed to prevent dynamic analysis.

Malware may employ techniques to avoid execution in controlled environments like sandboxes or virtual machines.

Analysts can use environment manipulation, deception techniques, and sandbox detection bypasses to trick the malware into running within a controlled environment, allowing for dynamic analysis.

Behavioral analysis, which focuses on monitoring the malware's actions and interactions with the system, can help overcome anti-analysis measures.

By observing the malware's runtime behavior, analysts can gather valuable insights into its actions and intentions.

This can include monitoring file system modifications, registry changes, network communications, and process interactions.

However, analysts should be cautious when conducting behavioral analysis, as some malware may exhibit delayed or limited malicious behavior to avoid detection.

To effectively overcome anti-analysis measures, analysts often employ a combination of static and dynamic analysis techniques. Static analysis involves examining the code without executing it, focusing on identifying patterns, logic, and data structures.

This can be done using disassemblers and decompilers to transform machine code into a more human-readable format.

Dynamic analysis, on the other hand, involves running the malware in a controlled environment and monitoring its behavior.

During dynamic analysis, analysts can use tools like Process Monitor, Wireshark, and CaptureBAT to record system events and interactions.

Additionally, analysts can employ automated analysis tools and sandboxes that specialize in executing and analyzing suspicious files while evading anti-analysis measures.

Collaboration among malware analysts and researchers is also a valuable approach to overcoming anti-analysis measures.

Sharing insights, strategies, and tools for anti-analysis evasion can lead to more effective analysis and a faster understanding of the malware's behavior.

Furthermore, the cybersecurity community often collaborates to identify and document new anti-analysis techniques and trends, enabling analysts to stay informed and adapt their approaches accordingly.

In summary, overcoming anti-analysis measures is a challenging yet crucial aspect of malware analysis and reverse engineering.

Malware authors employ various tactics to evade detection and hinder analysis, making it essential for cybersecurity professionals and researchers to employ a combination of technical expertise, creative problem-solving, and collaborative efforts.

By mastering the art of evasion and continuously adapting to evolving anti-analysis techniques, analysts can enhance their ability to dissect and understand malware effectively, contributing to improved cybersecurity and threat mitigation efforts.

Chapter 7: Reverse Engineering Malicious Network Protocols

Analyzing malware network traffic is a critical aspect of cybersecurity and malware analysis.

When malware infects a system, it often establishes communication with remote servers or command and control (C2) infrastructure.

Analyzing this network traffic can provide valuable insights into the malware's behavior, intentions, and potential threats to the affected system and network.

Understanding how to analyze malware network traffic is essential for cybersecurity professionals and analysts.

One of the first steps in analyzing malware network traffic is capturing the network packets generated by the infected system.

Packet capture tools like Wireshark or Tcpdump can intercept and record network traffic, allowing analysts to examine the data packets exchanged between the infected system and external servers.

By capturing this traffic, analysts can gain a deeper understanding of the malware's communication patterns and the information it sends and receives.

When analyzing network traffic, it's crucial to focus on the following key aspects:

Communication Protocols: Identifying the communication protocols used by the malware is essential. Malware often uses HTTP, HTTPS, DNS, or custom protocols to communicate with remote servers.

Destination Addresses: Determining the IP addresses or domain names of the remote servers that the malware communicates with is vital for tracking down malicious infrastructure.

Payload Analysis: Analyzing the content of network packets can reveal the data transmitted by the malware. This may include stolen information, commands from the C2 server, or other malicious activities.

Encryption and Encoding: Malware often encrypts or encodes its network traffic to obfuscate its communications. Deciphering these techniques is essential for understanding the content of the traffic.

Communication Patterns: Observing the frequency and timing of network communications can help identify patterns in the malware's behavior. This can provide insights into when the malware is active and what it's doing.

To analyze malware network traffic effectively, analysts can follow a systematic approach:

Packet Capture: Begin by capturing network traffic from the infected system. Ensure that the capture includes both incoming and outgoing traffic.

Traffic Analysis: Use network analysis tools like Wireshark to examine the captured packets. Sort and filter the traffic to focus on the relevant communication channels.

Protocol Identification: Identify the protocols used in the network traffic. Determine if the malware communicates over standard or custom protocols.

Destination Analysis: Investigate the destination addresses and domain names to understand where the malware is communicating. This may involve performing DNS lookups and IP geolocation.

Payload Examination: Analyze the payload of network packets to decipher the content. This can include decoding encoded data, decrypting encrypted traffic, and extracting any relevant information.

Behavior Profiling: Create a profile of the malware's network behavior. Document the communication patterns, timing, and frequency of network traffic.

Threat Intelligence: Cross-reference the identified domains and IP addresses with threat intelligence feeds to determine if they are associated with known malicious activity.

Command and Control (C2) Analysis: If the malware communicates with a C2 server, monitor the commands sent by the server and the responses from the infected system.

Malicious Payloads: If the network traffic includes payloads, analyze them for malware delivery, data exfiltration, or other malicious activities.

Reporting: Document your findings in a detailed report, including information about the malware's network behavior, communication channels, and potential threats.

Analyzing malware network traffic requires a combination of technical skills, network knowledge, and the ability to interpret data effectively.

It is essential to maintain a secure and isolated analysis environment to prevent the malware from causing further harm during analysis.

Furthermore, malware analysts must stay updated on evolving communication techniques and encryption methods used by malware to adapt their analysis strategies accordingly.

In summary, analyzing malware network traffic is a crucial aspect of cybersecurity and malware analysis.

Understanding the protocols, destinations, payloads, and behavior of malware's network communications is essential for identifying threats, tracking malicious infrastructure, and mitigating potential risks to affected systems and networks.

By following a systematic analysis approach and staying informed about evolving malware tactics, cybersecurity professionals and analysts can effectively analyze and respond to malware-related network threats.

Deciphering encrypted communications is a complex but crucial aspect of cybersecurity and malware analysis.
When malware communicates with remote servers or command and control infrastructure, it often encrypts the data to protect it from interception and analysis.
Decrypting these communications is essential for understanding the malware's behavior, extracting critical information, and responding effectively to the threat.
To decipher encrypted communications, analysts must possess a deep understanding of encryption algorithms, cryptographic techniques, and the specific encryption methods employed by the malware.
Encryption is a process of converting plain text or data into a ciphered format using an encryption algorithm and a cryptographic key.
The resulting ciphered text is unreadable without the appropriate decryption key.
Malware authors often use encryption to obfuscate their communication channels, making it challenging for security professionals to intercept and interpret the transmitted data.
One common encryption technique used by malware is the use of HTTPS (Hypertext Transfer Protocol Secure) for communication.
HTTPS encrypts the data transmitted between the malware and remote servers using the Transport Layer Security (TLS) or its predecessor, Secure Sockets Layer (SSL).
Decrypting HTTPS traffic requires knowledge of the TLS/SSL protocol and access to the encryption keys used during the communication.

Another encryption method employed by malware is custom encryption or encoding schemes.

Malware authors may develop their own encryption algorithms or use well-known encoding techniques to protect the transmitted data.

Decrypting such traffic requires reverse engineering and analysis of the encryption or encoding logic used by the malware.

In some cases, malware may employ strong encryption algorithms, making decryption a highly challenging task.

To decipher encrypted communications effectively, analysts can follow these steps:

Packet Capture: Capture network traffic between the infected system and remote servers or C2 infrastructure.

Traffic Analysis: Analyze the encrypted network packets to determine the encryption method used. Identify patterns that may reveal the presence of encryption.

Key Acquisition: Obtain the encryption keys or certificates used in the communication. This may involve extracting keys from the malware or compromised systems.

Decrypting TLS/SSL Traffic: For HTTPS traffic, if the private key used for encryption is available, analysts can use it to decrypt the SSL/TLS-encrypted data.

Custom Encryption Analysis: Reverse engineer the malware to understand the custom encryption or encoding logic. Identify key generation and decryption routines within the malware.

Decryption Tools: Develop or use specialized decryption tools or scripts to apply the acquired keys or decryption logic to the encrypted data.

Payload Analysis: Once the data is decrypted, analyze the content to extract information about the malware's behavior, commands, or any sensitive data being transmitted.

Behavioral Analysis: Observe how the decrypted data contributes to the malware's behavior and goals. This can include identifying malicious commands or data exfiltration.

Reporting: Document the decryption process and its findings in a detailed report, including information about the encryption methods used and decrypted content.

Deciphering encrypted communications is a challenging task that often requires a combination of technical skills, reverse engineering expertise, and access to encryption keys or certificates.

In some cases, cybersecurity professionals may need to collaborate with encryption experts or utilize specialized decryption tools and resources.

Additionally, maintaining a secure and isolated analysis environment is crucial to prevent further harm or exposure to the malware during decryption attempts.

Moreover, analysts should stay updated on evolving encryption techniques and encryption-breaking methods used by malware to adapt their decryption strategies accordingly.

In summary, deciphering encrypted communications is a critical skill in the field of cybersecurity and malware analysis.

Understanding encryption algorithms and techniques, acquiring decryption keys, and applying reverse engineering skills are essential for unraveling the mysteries hidden within encrypted malware communications.

By decrypting these communications, cybersecurity professionals can gain valuable insights into malware behavior, detect threats, and respond effectively to protect systems and networks.

Chapter 8: Memory Forensics and Malware Detection

Memory analysis tools and approaches play a vital role in cybersecurity and digital forensics, enabling experts to investigate and extract valuable information from a system's volatile memory.

Memory analysis is the process of examining a computer's RAM (Random Access Memory) to uncover evidence of malicious activities, system anomalies, and unauthorized access.

In the realm of cybersecurity, understanding memory analysis tools and techniques is crucial for incident response, malware analysis, and digital forensics investigations.

Memory analysis allows experts to identify running processes, discover hidden malware, uncover data remnants, and reconstruct events that occurred on a compromised system.

One common approach to memory analysis involves using specialized tools to acquire and analyze memory dumps, which are snapshots of a system's RAM at a specific point in time.

These memory dumps can be obtained using tools like Volatility, LiME (Linux Memory Extractor), or DumpIt for Windows systems.

Once a memory dump is obtained, analysts can employ various memory analysis techniques and tools to extract valuable information.

One essential memory analysis tool is Volatility, an open-source framework designed for analyzing memory dumps from various operating systems.

Volatility supports Windows, Linux, and macOS memory analysis and provides a wide range of plugins to extract information about processes, network connections, registry hives, and more.

With Volatility, analysts can identify running processes, detect rootkits and hidden processes, and recover deleted or encrypted data from memory.

Another important tool is Rekall, an open-source memory analysis framework that extends the capabilities of Volatility. Rekall offers improved support for both Windows and Linux memory analysis, making it a valuable resource for analysts working with diverse systems.

Rekall provides advanced memory analysis features, including the ability to analyze hibernation files, extract user credentials, and recover data from specific memory regions.

Additionally, the tool supports the analysis of virtual machine memory, making it useful for incident response and forensics in virtualized environments.

To approach memory analysis effectively, analysts must follow a systematic methodology:

Memory Acquisition: Obtain a memory dump from the target system using appropriate tools or techniques, ensuring that the dump captures the entire RAM contents.

Preliminary Analysis: Perform a preliminary examination of the memory dump to identify suspicious or anomalous artifacts, such as rogue processes, suspicious drivers, or signs of malware activity.

Process Analysis: Analyze the memory dump to identify running processes, their memory allocations, and execution threads. Look for signs of process injection or code execution in memory.

Malware Detection: Use memory analysis to detect and analyze malware in memory, including rootkits, Trojans, and other malicious code hiding within running processes.

Network Connections: Examine network-related data in memory to identify active network connections, open ports, and communication patterns. Determine if the system is compromised or involved in malicious activities.

User Activity: Extract user-related information, including user credentials, passwords, and tokens from memory, to investigate user interactions and potential breaches.

Persistence Mechanisms: Identify and analyze persistence mechanisms such as registry modifications, scheduled tasks, and autostart entries to understand how malware maintains persistence on the system.

Memory Forensics Reports: Document findings in detailed memory forensics reports, including evidence, artifacts, and analysis results. These reports may be used in legal proceedings or incident response efforts.

Cross-Platform Analysis: When dealing with mixed environments, adapt memory analysis techniques and tools to work with different operating systems to ensure comprehensive investigation.

Continuous Learning: Stay updated with the latest memory analysis tools and techniques, as adversaries continuously evolve their tactics to evade detection.

Memory analysis tools and approaches are indispensable in the world of cybersecurity and digital forensics.

They empower experts to dissect volatile memory, uncover threats, and piece together the puzzle of a compromised system or incident.

By mastering memory analysis techniques and using specialized tools, cybersecurity professionals can strengthen their capabilities in incident response, malware analysis, and forensic investigations, ultimately contributing to enhanced security and threat mitigation.

Detecting malware in system memory is a critical aspect of cybersecurity and malware analysis.

Malicious software often resides in a computer's RAM (Random Access Memory) to execute its code and carry out malicious activities.

System memory is volatile, meaning that its contents are lost when the computer is powered off, making it an attractive location for malware to hide and operate.

Detecting malware in system memory requires a comprehensive approach that involves scanning, monitoring, and analyzing the RAM to identify anomalous behavior and potentially malicious processes.

One common method for detecting malware in memory is the use of antivirus and anti-malware software.

These security tools employ signature-based and behavior-based detection techniques to identify known malware and suspicious activities.

Signature-based detection relies on a database of known malware signatures or patterns, while behavior-based detection looks for abnormal behavior that may indicate malware activity.

When a system is scanned with antivirus software, the tool examines the memory for any processes or code that match known malware signatures or exhibit unusual behavior.

If a match is found, the antivirus software can quarantine or remove the detected malware.

However, signature-based detection has limitations, as it can only detect known malware and may miss new or sophisticated threats that have not yet been cataloged.

To address this limitation, behavior-based detection techniques are employed to identify malicious activity patterns, such as code injection, memory manipulation, or process hijacking.

These behavioral indicators are often used to detect previously unknown or zero-day malware.

In addition to traditional antivirus and anti-malware solutions, memory analysis tools and techniques are essential for detecting malware in system memory.

Memory analysis involves examining the contents of the RAM to identify malicious processes, code injection, rootkits, and other signs of malware presence.

Tools like Volatility and Rekall are widely used for memory analysis and can provide valuable insights into memory-based malware.

Volatility, for example, allows analysts to extract information about running processes, network connections, open files, and more from memory dumps.

This information can help detect malware activity and identify compromised systems.

Memory analysis is particularly useful for uncovering advanced and persistent threats that may go undetected by traditional security software.

Memory forensics is another approach to detecting malware in system memory.

Forensic experts use memory forensics techniques to collect and analyze memory dumps, reconstructing the events that occurred on a compromised system.

Memory forensics can help identify malware execution, privilege escalation, and data exfiltration from memory.

To effectively detect malware in system memory, it's essential to follow a systematic approach:

Memory Capture: Obtain a memory dump of the target system using memory acquisition tools like LiME or DumpIt.

Preliminary Analysis: Perform an initial analysis of the memory dump to identify suspicious processes, loaded modules, and potential malware indicators.

Process Examination: Focus on the examination of running processes in memory, looking for signs of code injection, hidden processes, or malicious behavior.

Memory Artifacts: Explore memory artifacts, such as open network connections, loaded drivers, and user activity, to identify unusual or malicious activity.

Malware Signatures: Utilize known malware signatures or behavioral indicators to identify and confirm the presence of malware in memory.

Memory Forensics: Apply memory forensics techniques to reconstruct events and establish a timeline of activities involving the malware.

Reporting: Document findings in detailed reports, including evidence of malware in memory, analysis results, and recommendations for remediation.

Detecting malware in system memory is a continuous process, as new threats and attack techniques continually emerge.

Cybersecurity professionals must stay informed about the latest malware trends and invest in robust detection tools and memory analysis skills to effectively identify and respond to memory-resident malware.

By combining antivirus solutions, memory analysis tools, and memory forensics techniques, organizations can enhance their ability to detect and mitigate threats hiding in system memory, ultimately strengthening their cybersecurity posture.

Chapter 9: Advanced Malware Analysis Techniques

Advanced behavioral analysis is a sophisticated and powerful technique used in cybersecurity and malware analysis to detect and mitigate complex threats.

It goes beyond traditional signature-based detection methods, focusing on understanding the behavior of software and systems to identify malicious or abnormal activities.

This approach is particularly effective against zero-day attacks and polymorphic malware that frequently change their code to evade detection.

Advanced behavioral analysis leverages a range of techniques and technologies to monitor and analyze the actions and interactions of software and users within an environment.

One key component of this approach is sandboxing, where suspicious files or applications are executed in a controlled, isolated environment to observe their behavior.

Sandboxing allows security experts to assess how a program behaves when it runs, looking for any signs of malicious intent or unauthorized activities.

Advanced behavioral analysis also involves the monitoring of network traffic and system logs to detect unusual or suspicious patterns that may indicate a security threat.

Machine learning and artificial intelligence algorithms play a significant role in enhancing the capabilities of behavioral analysis.

These algorithms can analyze large datasets, identify anomalies, and predict potential security incidents based on historical data.

Behavioral analysis tools and systems can automatically detect and respond to emerging threats, reducing the reliance on manual investigation and human intervention.

One of the advantages of advanced behavioral analysis is its ability to detect new and unknown threats, including zero-day exploits and previously unseen malware variants.

By focusing on behavior rather than known signatures, this approach can identify malicious actions based on their characteristics, such as attempts to steal data, propagate to other systems, or establish unauthorized connections.

Another key aspect of advanced behavioral analysis is the use of heuristics and rules to define what constitutes normal or legitimate behavior in an environment.

Security experts can create custom rules or policies that specify the expected behavior of applications, users, and systems.

When deviations from these norms are detected, alerts or automated responses can be triggered to investigate potential threats.

Behavioral analysis is not limited to monitoring software behavior alone; it can also assess user behavior to detect insider threats or compromised accounts.

By analyzing user actions and access patterns, security teams can identify unusual login attempts, privilege escalation, or data exfiltration attempts.

Advanced behavioral analysis can help organizations reduce false positives by fine-tuning the rules and heuristics used in their security solutions.

This ensures that only genuine security threats are flagged for investigation, reducing the workload on security teams.

To implement effective advanced behavioral analysis, organizations should consider the following steps:

Data Collection: Collect and centralize data from various sources, including network traffic, system logs, application behavior, and user activities.

Baseline Establishment: Establish a baseline of normal behavior by analyzing historical data and defining rules and heuristics that characterize legitimate actions.

Anomaly Detection: Employ machine learning and AI algorithms to detect deviations from the established baseline, signaling potential security incidents.

Automated Responses: Implement automated responses to certain types of anomalies or threats, such as isolating compromised systems, blocking malicious IP addresses, or alerting security personnel.

Continuous Monitoring: Continuously monitor the network, systems, and user behavior to detect emerging threats and respond proactively.

Threat Intelligence Integration: Integrate threat intelligence feeds to stay updated on the latest threat indicators and enhance behavioral analysis capabilities.

Incident Investigation: When an alert is triggered, conduct thorough investigations to understand the nature and impact of the security incident.

Remediation: Based on investigation findings, take appropriate remediation actions to contain and eliminate the threat, and apply lessons learned to improve the security posture.

Regular Updates: Regularly update and fine-tune the rules and heuristics used for behavioral analysis to adapt to evolving threats and changes in the environment.

Training and Awareness: Provide training and awareness programs to educate employees and security teams about the importance of behavioral analysis and how to respond to alerts.

In summary, advanced behavioral analysis is a crucial component of modern cybersecurity strategies.

By focusing on behavior rather than relying solely on signatures, organizations can effectively detect and respond to a wide range of security threats, including those that have not been seen before.

With the aid of machine learning, AI, and automation, advanced behavioral analysis can significantly enhance an organization's ability to protect its digital assets and sensitive information from evolving threats in today's dynamic cybersecurity landscape. Advanced code analysis techniques are essential tools in the arsenal of cybersecurity experts and software developers alike, enabling them to gain a deeper understanding of complex software systems, identify vulnerabilities, and enhance overall code quality.

These techniques go beyond basic code review and static analysis, delving into the intricate details of a program's behavior, structure, and potential security flaws. One of the fundamental aspects of advanced code analysis is dynamic analysis, a process that involves executing the software and observing its behavior in real-time.

Dynamic analysis tools, such as debuggers and dynamic code analyzers, allow analysts to step through a program's execution, inspect variable values, and identify runtime errors or security vulnerabilities.

Dynamic analysis provides invaluable insights into how a program interacts with its environment, handles data, and responds to various inputs.

Another advanced technique is taint analysis, which tracks the flow of data within a program to identify potential security issues.

In taint analysis, data is marked as "tainted" when it originates from untrusted sources, and its propagation is traced throughout the codebase.

By monitoring how tainted data is used and whether it reaches sensitive operations or resources, analysts can pinpoint potential security weaknesses, such as data injection or manipulation vulnerabilities.

Control flow analysis is another powerful method used in advanced code analysis.

This technique examines how control flows through a program, helping identify code paths, conditional branches, loops, and potential execution anomalies.

Control flow analysis can uncover issues like unreachable code, deadlocks, or improper handling of exceptional situations, improving code reliability and security.

Abstract interpretation is a mathematical approach to code analysis that allows for the automatic discovery of program properties.

By modeling the program's behavior symbolically and applying abstract domains, abstract interpretation can uncover subtle security flaws, such as buffer overflows, data races, or violations of security policies.

Symbolic execution is yet another advanced technique that explores different code paths by symbolically executing the program with inputs represented as symbols.

Symbolic execution can help identify path-sensitive vulnerabilities, such as input validation errors, path traversal issues, or unintended information disclosure.

Static analysis tools that incorporate abstract interpretation or symbolic execution techniques can significantly enhance the security and reliability of software.

Control and data flow analysis, along with abstract interpretation, play a crucial role in discovering security vulnerabilities, optimizing code, and ensuring that a program behaves as intended.

Advanced code analysis techniques also extend to the realm of binary analysis, where analysts examine compiled executable code without access to the original source code.

Binary analysis tools and reverse engineering techniques allow experts to understand the inner workings of closed-source software, identify security flaws, and develop patches or workarounds.

Intricate analysis of assembly code, disassembled binaries, and debugging information can reveal vulnerabilities that threat actors might exploit.

To succeed in advanced code analysis, experts often rely on interactive disassemblers and decompilers that translate binary code into more understandable representations.

These tools help analysts reverse engineer software, analyze control and data flow, and identify weaknesses or undocumented features.

Fuzz testing, or fuzzing, is a dynamic analysis technique used to find vulnerabilities by injecting malformed or unexpected data into a program.

Fuzzing tools systematically test how a program handles various inputs, uncovering memory corruption issues, crashes, or unexpected behaviors that could be potential security risks.

Advanced fuzzing techniques, such as feedback-driven fuzzing and hybrid fuzzing, improve the efficiency of vulnerability discovery by guiding the generation of test cases based on program responses.

Beyond finding vulnerabilities, advanced code analysis techniques also contribute to code quality and maintainability.

Code metrics, cyclomatic complexity analysis, and static code analysis tools can identify code smells, maintainability issues, and potential sources of technical debt.

By addressing these concerns early in the development process, software engineers can produce more robust and secure code.

Incorporating security-focused coding practices, such as secure coding guidelines and security design patterns, is another essential aspect of advanced code analysis.

Security-focused coding practices help developers proactively address common security pitfalls, such as input validation, authentication, authorization, and data protection.

These practices align with security standards, reduce the risk of security vulnerabilities, and foster a security-conscious development culture.

In summary, advanced code analysis techniques are indispensable tools for cybersecurity professionals, software developers, and reverse engineers.

These techniques encompass dynamic analysis, taint analysis, control flow analysis, abstract interpretation, symbolic execution, binary analysis, and fuzz testing.

By applying these techniques, experts can uncover security vulnerabilities, enhance code quality, and gain a deeper understanding of complex software systems.

Moreover, these practices contribute to the development of more secure, reliable, and maintainable software, ultimately reducing the exposure to cyber threats and ensuring the integrity of critical applications.

Chapter 10: Case Studies in Complex Malware Analysis

In-depth analysis of real-world malware is a fundamental aspect of cybersecurity research and defense strategies.

It provides valuable insights into the tactics, techniques, and procedures used by malicious actors, helping security professionals understand the evolving threat landscape.

Real-world malware is a term that encompasses a wide range of malicious software, including viruses, worms, Trojans, ransomware, spyware, and rootkits, among others.

Each type of malware has its own unique characteristics and capabilities, making it essential to conduct thorough analysis to determine its behavior and impact.

Analyzing real-world malware often starts with the collection of malware samples from various sources, such as honeypots, malware repositories, or incident response engagements.

These samples serve as the basis for further investigation and research.

The first step in the analysis process is to isolate the malware sample in a controlled and isolated environment, commonly referred to as a sandbox.

Sandboxing provides a safe and controlled space for executing the malware, allowing analysts to observe its behavior without compromising the host system.

Once isolated, the malware can be executed and monitored to gather information about its activities.

Dynamic analysis, which involves monitoring the malware's behavior during execution, is a crucial technique in understanding real-world malware.

This analysis provides insights into the malware's capabilities, such as its propagation methods, file system interactions, network communications, and evasion techniques.

By observing the malware's behavior, analysts can determine its intended purpose, whether it's stealing sensitive data, encrypting files for ransom, or establishing a foothold for further attacks.

Network traffic analysis is another vital component of in-depth malware analysis.

By capturing and dissecting the network traffic generated by the malware, analysts can identify command-and-control servers, communication protocols, and data exfiltration techniques.

This information is invaluable for tracking the malware's infrastructure and preventing further infections.

During the analysis process, researchers often examine the malware's code, either by reverse engineering the binary or decompiling it.

This step allows analysts to gain a deeper understanding of the malware's functionality, encryption methods, and obfuscation techniques.

Reverse engineering can reveal vulnerabilities and weaknesses in the malware's design, which may be exploited to develop countermeasures or antivirus signatures.

Static analysis, which involves examining the malware's code without executing it, can also provide insights into its functionality and potential indicators of compromise (IoCs).

By analyzing the code, researchers can identify strings, functions, and API calls that are characteristic of the malware's behavior.

The combination of dynamic and static analysis techniques enables analysts to create a comprehensive profile of the real-world malware, which can be used for detection and prevention.

Advanced malware analysis tools and sandboxes offer automation capabilities, which streamline the analysis process by capturing and aggregating data points related to the malware's behavior.

These tools provide visual representations of the malware's execution flow, network traffic patterns, and system interactions, aiding analysts in identifying malicious activities more efficiently.

In addition to examining the technical aspects of malware, in-depth analysis may also involve tracking the threat actor behind the malware.

This can include identifying the malware's origin, determining the attacker's motivations, and establishing attribution.

Attribution is a complex and challenging task that may involve correlating indicators from multiple sources, such as IP addresses, malware families, and attack infrastructure.

Threat intelligence sharing within the cybersecurity community plays a crucial role in uncovering the origins of real-world malware and understanding the broader threat landscape.

Once the in-depth analysis is complete, security professionals can use the gathered insights to develop and implement mitigation strategies.

This may involve updating antivirus signatures, creating network rules to block malicious traffic, or patching vulnerabilities exploited by the malware.

Additionally, the findings from real-world malware analysis contribute to threat intelligence databases, enhancing the collective knowledge of the cybersecurity community.

Sharing information about new malware variants, attack techniques, and IoCs helps organizations across various industries defend against similar threats.

Furthermore, the results of in-depth malware analysis can be used to educate security professionals, incident responders, and threat hunters on the evolving tactics employed by threat actors.

Training programs and awareness initiatives based on real-world examples empower security teams to better detect, respond to, and mitigate malware threats.

In summary, in-depth analysis of real-world malware is a critical component of cybersecurity efforts.

It involves isolating and observing malware samples, conducting dynamic and static analysis, examining network traffic, and, in some cases, attributing the threat to specific actors or groups.

The insights gained from this analysis aid in developing effective countermeasures, enhancing threat intelligence, and educating security professionals.

As the threat landscape continues to evolve, the importance of in-depth malware analysis remains paramount in protecting organizations and individuals from malicious software and cyberattacks.

Expert insights from complex malware case studies offer a unique and invaluable perspective into the world of cybersecurity, revealing the intricate strategies employed by threat actors and the challenges faced by security professionals.

These case studies delve deep into real-world incidents, dissecting the malware, tactics, and techniques used in sophisticated attacks.

By examining these complex cases, security experts gain a deeper understanding of evolving threats and develop more effective defense strategies.

Complex malware case studies often begin with an overview of the incident, providing context and background information about the attack.

This includes details such as the target organization, the initial attack vector, and the timeline of events leading up to the discovery of the malware.

Understanding the context is crucial for unraveling the full story behind the attack and its potential impact.

The malware analysis in these case studies is not limited to technical aspects but also includes an examination of the threat actor's motivations and objectives.

By profiling the attacker, security experts can gain insights into their goals, whether they are financial gain, espionage, or disruption of operations.

Analyzing the malware's code and behavior is a fundamental part of complex case studies, as it reveals the intricacies of the threat.

Security researchers often reverse engineer the malware, dissecting its binary code to uncover vulnerabilities, evasion techniques, and data exfiltration methods.

This in-depth analysis is critical for understanding how the malware operates and how it may have evaded detection.

Complex malware often employs advanced techniques to evade traditional security measures, such as antivirus software or intrusion detection systems.

Case studies highlight these evasion tactics, shedding light on how threat actors adapt and evolve their strategies to bypass defenses.

The study of complex malware also includes an examination of the malware's propagation methods.

This can involve the exploitation of software vulnerabilities, social engineering, or the use of zero-day exploits.

Understanding how the malware spreads within an organization is crucial for preventing further infections and mitigating the impact.

Complex malware case studies often reveal the use of sophisticated command-and-control (C2) infrastructure.

Security experts trace the malware's communication channels, identifying the C2 servers and protocols used to communicate with the attacker.

This information is vital for organizations to block malicious traffic and sever the malware's connection to its controller.

An important aspect of complex malware case studies is the analysis of data exfiltration methods.

Threat actors often seek to steal sensitive data, and understanding how they exfiltrate this data is essential for protecting valuable assets.

This may involve the use of encryption, covert channels, or other techniques to bypass data loss prevention measures.

Mitigation strategies and lessons learned are a crucial part of complex malware case studies.

Security experts analyze the incident response efforts, highlighting what worked well and where improvements could have been made.

These insights help organizations fine-tune their incident response plans and enhance their overall cybersecurity posture.

Complex malware case studies also underscore the importance of threat intelligence sharing and collaboration within the cybersecurity community.

By sharing information about emerging threats and attack techniques, organizations can better prepare and defend against similar incidents.

Expert insights from complex malware case studies provide a wealth of knowledge that can benefit organizations of all sizes.

These case studies offer a window into the evolving tactics and strategies employed by threat actors, helping security professionals stay one step ahead.

By learning from real-world incidents, organizations can better protect their systems, data, and reputation.

Additionally, these case studies emphasize the need for continuous monitoring, proactive threat hunting, and a robust incident response plan to detect and mitigate complex malware attacks.

In summary, complex malware case studies offer a comprehensive and insightful view of the ever-changing cybersecurity landscape.

These studies provide a deep dive into real-world incidents, dissecting the malware, tactics, and techniques used by threat actors.

By analyzing these cases, security experts gain valuable insights that can inform defense strategies, improve incident response, and enhance overall cybersecurity readiness.

The knowledge gained from these case studies empowers organizations to better protect themselves against complex malware threats and adapt to the evolving threat landscape.

BOOK 4
ADVANCED TECHNIQUES IN MALWARE REVERSE
ENGINEERING
EXPERT-LEVEL INSIGHTS

ROB BOTWRIGHT

Chapter 1: Mastering the Art of Advanced Malware Analysis

Advanced malware analysis tools and techniques are indispensable resources in the ongoing battle against sophisticated cyber threats, providing security professionals with the means to dissect, understand, and ultimately mitigate complex malware attacks.

These tools and techniques have evolved significantly in response to the growing complexity and diversity of malware, enabling analysts to uncover the inner workings of malicious software and develop effective countermeasures.

Dynamic analysis tools play a pivotal role in advanced malware analysis, allowing analysts to observe the behavior of malware in real-time.

Sandbox environments, which isolate and emulate the execution of malware, provide a controlled setting for dynamic analysis.

By executing malware within these sandboxes, analysts can monitor its actions, record system interactions, and detect malicious behavior, such as file system changes, network communications, and attempts to evade detection.

In addition to sandboxes, dynamic analysis tools include debuggers, which allow analysts to step through the execution of malware, inspect memory, and analyze code flow.

Dynamic analysis not only reveals the malware's behavior but also provides insights into its functionality, capabilities, and potential impact on the target system.

Static analysis techniques complement dynamic analysis by examining the malware's code and structure without executing it.

Static analysis tools, such as disassemblers and decompilers, transform the binary code of malware into a more human-readable form, enabling analysts to scrutinize the code for vulnerabilities, obfuscation techniques, and malicious logic.

This method of analysis unveils the malware's inner workings and helps identify potential security flaws that may be exploited for defense.

Taint analysis is an advanced technique that tracks the flow of data within a program, allowing analysts to identify how inputs from untrusted sources propagate through the code and potentially influence sensitive operations.

By monitoring the path of tainted data, analysts can uncover vulnerabilities related to data injection, manipulation, or misuse.

Control flow analysis is another critical aspect of advanced malware analysis, focusing on understanding how a program's control flow is influenced by various conditions, loops, and branches.

Control flow analysis helps identify vulnerabilities stemming from incorrect program behavior, such as deadlocks, unreachable code, and improper error handling.

Abstract interpretation is a mathematical approach to code analysis that aims to automatically discover program properties and verify their correctness.

By symbolically modeling the program's behavior and applying abstract domains, abstract interpretation can detect subtle security flaws like buffer overflows, data races, and violations of security policies.

Symbolic execution is a technique that explores different code paths by symbolically executing the program with inputs represented as symbols rather than concrete values.

Symbolic execution can uncover path-sensitive vulnerabilities, such as input validation errors, path traversal issues, and unintended information disclosure.

Binary analysis is essential when dealing with closed-source or compiled software.

Analysts use reverse engineering techniques and specialized tools to examine compiled executable code, gain insights into the malware's functionality, and identify vulnerabilities.

Interactive disassemblers and decompilers are valuable tools that translate binary code into more human-readable representations, aiding analysts in understanding the malware's operation.

Fuzz testing, or fuzzing, is a dynamic analysis technique that involves injecting malformed or unexpected data into a program to uncover vulnerabilities.

Fuzzing tools systematically test how a program handles various inputs, exposing memory corruption issues, crashes, or unexpected behaviors that could be exploited by attackers.

Advanced fuzzing techniques, such as feedback-driven fuzzing and hybrid fuzzing, enhance the efficiency of vulnerability discovery by generating test cases based on the program's responses.

Advanced malware analysis tools often offer automation capabilities that streamline the analysis process by capturing and aggregating data related to the malware's behavior.

These tools provide visual representations of execution flow, network traffic patterns, and system interactions, making it easier for analysts to identify malicious activities efficiently.

In addition to dissecting the malware itself, advanced analysis encompasses the examination of the malware's network communications.

Analysts capture and analyze the network traffic generated by the malware to identify command-and-control (C2) servers, communication protocols, and data exfiltration methods.

This information is vital for tracking the malware's infrastructure, severing its connections to the C2 servers, and preventing further infections.

The results of advanced malware analysis contribute to the development of detection signatures, intrusion detection rules, and threat intelligence feeds.

By sharing these findings with the cybersecurity community, organizations enhance collective knowledge and improve the overall defense against similar threats.

Advanced malware analysis also supports the development of mitigation strategies, enabling organizations to update antivirus signatures, create network rules to block malicious traffic, or patch vulnerabilities exploited by the malware.

Furthermore, the insights gained from advanced analysis can be used to educate security professionals, incident responders, and threat hunters on the evolving tactics used by threat actors.

Training programs and awareness initiatives based on real-world examples empower security teams to better detect, respond to, and mitigate malware threats effectively.

In summary, advanced malware analysis tools and techniques are essential components of modern cybersecurity, providing the means to dissect and understand complex malware attacks.

These tools encompass dynamic analysis, static analysis, taint analysis, control flow analysis, abstract interpretation, symbolic execution, binary analysis, and fuzz testing.

By applying these techniques, analysts can uncover security vulnerabilities, enhance code quality, and gain a deeper understanding of malware behavior.

Moreover, advanced analysis practices contribute to the development of more secure, reliable, and maintainable software, ultimately reducing the exposure to cyber threats and ensuring the integrity of critical applications.

Advanced behavioral analysis approaches are indispensable tools in the field of cybersecurity, providing organizations with the means to detect and respond to complex and evasive threats.

Traditional signature-based detection methods have limitations, and attackers constantly evolve their tactics, making it essential to adopt more advanced techniques to identify malicious behavior.

Behavioral analysis focuses on monitoring and analyzing the actions and activities of software and users within a network or system.

One of the key elements of advanced behavioral analysis is the creation of baseline profiles for normal system and user behavior.

This involves observing and recording typical actions, processes, and interactions within an environment over time.

By establishing these baselines, security analysts can identify deviations that may indicate suspicious or malicious activity.

Machine learning algorithms play a significant role in advanced behavioral analysis, as they can identify anomalies and patterns that may be indicative of threats.

Machine learning models are trained on historical data to recognize normal behavior, allowing them to flag unusual or potentially malicious activities.

These models continuously adapt and improve their accuracy as they encounter new data, making them highly effective in identifying emerging threats.

Endpoint detection and response (EDR) solutions leverage advanced behavioral analysis to monitor activities on individual endpoints, such as computers and mobile devices.

EDR solutions track processes, file changes, registry modifications, network connections, and user behavior to detect and respond to suspicious activities in real-time.

User and entity behavior analytics (UEBA) is another critical component of advanced behavioral analysis.

UEBA solutions track user behavior, login patterns, and access to resources to detect abnormal activities, such as unauthorized access or insider threats.

By analyzing user behavior, organizations can identify potential security risks and take proactive measures to mitigate them.

Network traffic analysis is an integral part of advanced behavioral analysis, as it focuses on monitoring the flow of data within a network.

By analyzing network traffic, security teams can detect unusual or suspicious patterns that may indicate a security breach or data exfiltration.

Advanced behavioral analysis solutions often integrate threat intelligence feeds to enrich their understanding of potential threats.

These feeds provide real-time information about known threats, malicious IP addresses, and indicators of compromise (IoCs).

By incorporating threat intelligence, organizations can enhance their ability to detect and respond to threats promptly.

Sandboxing is a technique used in advanced behavioral analysis to isolate and execute potentially malicious code in a controlled environment.

Sandbox environments mimic real systems but provide a safe space for analyzing code and observing its behavior.

By executing suspicious code in a sandbox, security analysts can monitor its actions and determine whether it exhibits malicious behavior.

Memory forensics is a crucial aspect of advanced behavioral analysis, as it involves examining the volatile memory of a system to identify malware, rootkits, and other malicious artifacts.

Memory forensics tools enable analysts to extract valuable information from a system's RAM, providing insights into the current state of a compromised system.

Machine learning models, such as anomaly detection algorithms, are applied to memory forensics data to identify irregularities that may indicate an intrusion.

Behavioral analysis is not limited to monitoring and analyzing the actions of software and users.

It also extends to analyzing the behavior of network traffic and devices.

Advanced network traffic analysis solutions can detect anomalies in traffic patterns, such as large data transfers, unusual port activity, or suspicious communication with known malicious domains.

By monitoring device behavior, organizations can identify compromised or vulnerable devices on their network.

Advanced behavioral analysis approaches also consider the human factor in cybersecurity.

Social engineering attacks, phishing attempts, and insider threats often rely on manipulating human behavior.

Organizations can deploy training and awareness programs to educate employees about cybersecurity best practices and to recognize and report suspicious activity.

Behavioral biometrics is an emerging field that leverages unique patterns in user behavior, such as typing speed, mouse movements, and touchscreen gestures, to authenticate users and detect impostors.

This technology adds an additional layer of security by verifying the user's identity based on their behavior.

Advanced behavioral analysis can be applied in real-time or retrospectively to investigate security incidents.

In retrospective analysis, security teams review historical data to identify patterns or activities that may have been missed initially.

This approach can help uncover past security breaches and improve incident response procedures.

In summary, advanced behavioral analysis approaches are essential for organizations looking to bolster their cybersecurity defenses against increasingly sophisticated threats.

These approaches encompass the monitoring and analysis of system behavior, user behavior, network traffic, and device behavior.

Machine learning, threat intelligence, EDR solutions, UEBA, network traffic analysis, sandboxing, memory forensics, and behavioral biometrics are key components of advanced behavioral analysis.

By leveraging these techniques, organizations can detect and respond to security threats effectively, protect their data and assets, and stay ahead of evolving cyber threats.

Chapter 2: Advanced Assembly Language and Code Analysis

In-depth assembly language instruction analysis is a crucial aspect of understanding the inner workings of computer programs and malware alike.

Assembly language is a low-level programming language that is closely tied to the architecture of a computer's central processing unit (CPU).

Each assembly language instruction corresponds to a specific machine language instruction that the CPU can execute directly.

Analyzing assembly language instructions involves dissecting the code at the lowest level to comprehend the precise sequence of operations performed by a program.

In assembly language, instructions are composed of mnemonics that represent fundamental operations such as addition, subtraction, branching, and data manipulation.

Mnemonics are human-readable symbols that provide a higher-level representation of the machine code instructions.

To begin an in-depth analysis of assembly language instructions, it is essential to have a deep understanding of the CPU architecture being used.

Different CPUs have distinct instruction sets and architectures, and analysis techniques may vary accordingly.

Common assembly languages include x86, ARM, MIPS, and PowerPC, each with its own set of instructions and addressing modes.

Once you have a grasp of the CPU architecture, the next step in assembly language analysis is disassembling the binary code.

Disassembling is the process of converting the binary code of a program into its equivalent assembly language instructions.

This step is crucial for human analysts, as it makes the code more readable and understandable.

Disassemblers are specialized tools designed to perform this task, generating assembly code that can be examined and analyzed.

During the disassembly process, the disassembler identifies memory addresses, labels, and operands, helping analysts make sense of the code's structure.

When conducting an in-depth analysis of assembly language instructions, it is important to identify entry points, which are locations in the code where execution begins.

Entry points often include functions, subroutines, or the main program itself.

Analyzing the flow of control within the code is a key aspect of assembly language instruction analysis.

This involves tracing how execution moves from one instruction to another, including conditional branches, loops, and function calls.

Control flow analysis helps uncover the program's logic and allows analysts to identify potential vulnerabilities or suspicious behavior.

In addition to control flow analysis, data flow analysis is another vital aspect of understanding assembly language instructions.

Data flow analysis tracks how data moves through the program, identifying variables, memory locations, and registers used to store and manipulate data.

By examining the data flow, analysts can gain insights into how information is processed and manipulated within the program.

Register usage is a critical element of assembly language instruction analysis.

Registers are small, fast storage locations within the CPU used to hold data temporarily during operations.

Understanding which registers are used for specific calculations or data storage is essential for comprehending the program's inner workings.

Moreover, analyzing how data is moved between registers and memory locations provides insights into data manipulation.

Stack analysis is particularly important in assembly language analysis, as the stack is frequently used for managing program execution and storing local variables.

Analyzing stack operations, such as pushes, pops, and stack frame manipulation, helps in understanding function calls, parameter passing, and variable storage.

To fully comprehend assembly language instructions, analysts must be familiar with addressing modes.

Addressing modes define how operands are specified in instructions and how data is accessed from memory or registers.

Common addressing modes include immediate, direct, indirect, indexed, and relative addressing.

By recognizing the addressing mode used in each instruction, analysts can deduce how data is accessed and manipulated.

Conditional jumps and branches are essential components of assembly language instructions, enabling programs to make decisions and execute different code paths based on specific conditions.

Analyzing conditional jumps and branches helps identify decision points and the conditions that influence program behavior.

In-depth assembly language instruction analysis often involves code optimization.

Optimization aims to improve program efficiency and performance by reducing redundant or unnecessary instructions.

This process may result in the transformation of code to be more compact and execute faster.

However, it is important to note that some forms of malware employ code obfuscation techniques to make analysis more challenging.

Obfuscated code intentionally complicates the analysis process by introducing misleading instructions, dead code, or encryption.

Reverse engineers and analysts must employ specialized techniques to deobfuscate such code and reveal its true functionality.

When analyzing assembly language instructions in the context of malware, it is essential to focus on identifying malicious behavior.

This includes the identification of code responsible for actions such as data theft, system exploitation, network communication, and evasion of security mechanisms.

Malware analysts often use dynamic analysis techniques, such as debugging and code execution in controlled environments, to observe how the malware behaves at runtime.

By comparing the observed behavior with the disassembled code, analysts can pinpoint the specific assembly language instructions responsible for malicious activities.

Furthermore, understanding assembly language instructions helps in developing detection and mitigation strategies for malware.

Security professionals can create signatures, rules, or behavioral indicators to identify and block malicious code based on the patterns identified during analysis.

In summary, in-depth assembly language instruction analysis is a fundamental skill in the field of reverse engineering and malware analysis.

It involves disassembling binary code, analyzing control and data flow, understanding register and stack usage, recognizing addressing modes, and identifying conditional jumps and branches.

Through meticulous analysis, security professionals can uncover the functionality of software, detect vulnerabilities, and combat malicious code effectively.

Advanced code analysis strategies are indispensable tools in the field of cybersecurity, enabling security professionals to dissect and understand complex software and malware.

Code analysis is the process of examining the source code or binary code of a program to gain insights into its functionality, behavior, and potential security vulnerabilities.

While basic code analysis techniques provide a foundation for understanding code, advanced strategies delve deeper into the intricacies of software, allowing for more comprehensive assessments.

One of the primary goals of advanced code analysis is to identify vulnerabilities and security weaknesses that could be exploited by attackers.

Code vulnerabilities, such as buffer overflows, race conditions, and input validation flaws, can pose significant risks to the security and stability of software systems.

Advanced code analysis tools and techniques can uncover these vulnerabilities, enabling organizations to patch or mitigate them before they can be exploited. Static code analysis is a critical component of advanced code analysis. Static analysis involves examining source code or binary code without executing the program, making it a valuable tool for identifying potential issues early in the development process.

Advanced static analysis tools can perform deep code inspection, checking for coding standards violations, security vulnerabilities, and code smells that may indicate poor design or potential issues.

Dynamic code analysis, on the other hand, involves analyzing code during runtime, simulating program execution to detect issues that may only manifest when the software is running. Advanced dynamic analysis tools can capture program execution traces, monitor system calls, and identify runtime errors, memory leaks, and resource usage patterns.

Fuzz testing, a dynamic analysis technique, involves providing unexpected or malicious inputs to a program to identify vulnerabilities and crashes.

Advanced fuzzing tools use intelligent algorithms and mutation strategies to generate input test cases that maximize code coverage and vulnerability discovery.

Symbolic execution is another advanced code analysis technique that explores all possible paths through a program's code by symbolically executing instructions and constraints.

This technique can identify complex vulnerabilities, such as logic flaws and program invariant violations, by exhaustively exploring code paths.

Taint analysis is an advanced technique that tracks the flow of data through a program, identifying sources of untrusted input and how that input propagates through the code.

Taint analysis can help uncover security vulnerabilities related to data leakage, injection attacks, and improper validation of input.

Control flow analysis is a crucial aspect of advanced code analysis, as it focuses on understanding how program control flows between different functions, modules, and libraries.

Analyzing control flow can help identify code paths that may lead to unauthorized access, privilege escalation, or code execution vulnerabilities. Advanced code analysis strategies also encompass binary code analysis, which involves examining compiled executables or libraries. Binary code analysis can reveal insights into third-party libraries, proprietary software, or malware for which source code is not available.

Disassembly tools and reverse engineering techniques are employed to transform binary code into human-readable assembly language, facilitating analysis.

Advanced binary analysis techniques can help uncover hidden functionality, encryption algorithms, and anti-analysis mechanisms employed by malicious software.

Malware analysis relies heavily on advanced code analysis strategies to understand the inner workings of malicious code.

Security researchers use dynamic analysis to observe malware behavior in controlled environments, while static analysis and disassembly are used to dissect the code and identify indicators of compromise.

Advanced code analysis can also assist in identifying evasion techniques used by malware to avoid detection and analysis.

Code obfuscation, packing, and anti-analysis tricks are commonly employed by malware authors, making it essential to employ advanced techniques to deobfuscate and uncover the true functionality of malicious code.

Code similarity analysis is another advanced technique used in cybersecurity to identify code reuse, plagiarism, or the presence of third-party components with known vulnerabilities.

By comparing code fragments or binaries to databases of known software, security professionals can identify potential security risks and enforce code integrity.

Advanced code analysis often involves the use of automated tools and scripts to streamline the analysis process.

These tools can perform code analysis at scale, identify common vulnerabilities, and generate reports that highlight security issues.

Security teams can then prioritize and address these issues to improve software security.

Machine learning and artificial intelligence play a growing role in advanced code analysis. These technologies can be used to develop predictive models that identify patterns of behavior or code that are indicative of security vulnerabilities.

Machine learning algorithms can also assist in classifying code as malicious or benign, helping security analysts make informed decisions quickly.

The importance of advanced code analysis extends beyond vulnerability identification; it is also critical for ensuring compliance with security standards and regulations. Many industries have established security standards and best practices that require code analysis as part of the development and testing process.

Advanced code analysis can help organizations meet these compliance requirements by identifying and addressing security issues.

Code review is a fundamental practice in software development, and advanced code analysis techniques can enhance this process significantly. Security professionals can use advanced analysis tools to perform code reviews that focus specifically on security-related concerns.

This ensures that code is not only functional but also secure, reducing the risk of security breaches.

In summary, advanced code analysis strategies are a vital component of cybersecurity and software development.

These strategies encompass static and dynamic analysis techniques, fuzz testing, symbolic execution, taint analysis, and control flow analysis.

They also extend to binary code analysis, code similarity analysis, and the use of automated tools and machine learning.

Advanced code analysis not only identifies vulnerabilities but also supports compliance efforts, enhances code reviews, and aids in understanding and mitigating security risks.

As technology continues to advance, the role of advanced code analysis in cybersecurity will only become more critical in protecting organizations from emerging threats.

Chapter 3: Exploiting Vulnerabilities in Malware

Identifying and exploiting vulnerabilities in malware is a complex and essential aspect of cybersecurity and malware analysis.

Vulnerabilities in malware can be thought of as weaknesses or flaws in the code or design of malicious software that can be leveraged for various purposes.

These vulnerabilities can exist due to programming errors, oversight by the malware author, or the inclusion of third-party components with known vulnerabilities.

Identifying vulnerabilities in malware requires a deep understanding of the malware's code, behavior, and underlying architecture.

It often involves reverse engineering and detailed analysis of the malware sample.

One common vulnerability in malware is poor input validation, where the malware fails to properly check or sanitize user inputs.

Exploiting this vulnerability might involve crafting specially crafted inputs that trigger unintended behavior in the malware, such as buffer overflows or code injection.

Another common vulnerability is the presence of hardcoded credentials or encryption keys within the malware.

By extracting these credentials, security researchers can gain access to command and control servers, decrypt communication, or even disrupt the malware's operations.

Vulnerabilities can also arise from the malware's interaction with the host system.

For example, if the malware relies on certain system calls or APIs that have known vulnerabilities or weaknesses, these can be exploited to manipulate the malware's execution or gather information about its activities.

Moreover, vulnerabilities in the malware's evasion techniques can be exploited.

Many malware strains use anti-analysis and obfuscation techniques to thwart security researchers.

Identifying flaws in these techniques can lead to more effective analysis and detection of the malware.

In some cases, vulnerabilities in malware may be intentionally placed by the malware author as a form of deception.

These "honeypot" vulnerabilities are designed to lure analysts into focusing on fake weaknesses while ignoring the malware's true capabilities.

Identifying and exploiting vulnerabilities in malware is a high-stakes game where security professionals strive to outsmart the malware authors.

However, it's crucial to note that the process must be carried out with caution, following ethical guidelines and legal regulations.

Exploiting vulnerabilities in malware is often a means to an end, such as gaining insights into the malware's inner workings or developing countermeasures.

Security researchers and analysts must prioritize responsible disclosure and collaboration with law enforcement to combat cyber threats effectively.

In some cases, vulnerabilities in malware can lead to the discovery of zero-day vulnerabilities in legitimate software.

This happens when malware exploits previously unknown vulnerabilities in the operating system or third-party software to gain a foothold on a system.

Identifying these vulnerabilities can have broader implications for system security, as they may need to be patched or mitigated to prevent future malware attacks.

Vulnerabilities in malware can be discovered through various means, including static and dynamic analysis.

Static analysis involves examining the malware's code and behavior without executing it.

Security researchers use disassembly tools and reverse engineering techniques to dissect the code and identify potential weaknesses.

Dynamic analysis, on the other hand, involves executing the malware in a controlled environment and monitoring its behavior.

By observing how the malware behaves during execution, analysts can uncover vulnerabilities related to its runtime activities and interactions with the system.

Fuzz testing is another technique used to identify vulnerabilities in malware.

By feeding the malware various inputs and monitoring its response, analysts can discover weaknesses related to input handling, parsing, and error handling.

Additionally, vulnerability scanners and analysis tools designed specifically for malware can aid in the detection of vulnerabilities.

Once vulnerabilities in malware are identified, security professionals must assess their potential impact and exploitability.

This involves evaluating the severity of the vulnerability, the conditions required for exploitation, and the potential consequences if exploited.

Assessment helps prioritize which vulnerabilities should be further investigated or reported.

Exploiting vulnerabilities in malware often requires crafting specialized exploits or payloads tailored to the specific weakness.

The goal is to trigger the vulnerability in a controlled manner to gather information or disrupt the malware's operations.

Security researchers may develop proof-of-concept exploits to demonstrate the impact of the vulnerability.

Exploitation can lead to valuable insights into the malware's capabilities and objectives.

However, it is essential to conduct exploitation in a controlled environment to prevent unintended consequences or damage to systems.

Moreover, responsible disclosure is critical when vulnerabilities are discovered.

Sharing findings with relevant authorities, such as law enforcement agencies and software vendors, helps protect potential victims and contributes to cybersecurity efforts.

In some cases, vulnerabilities in malware can be used to develop defensive measures and countermeasures.

For instance, understanding how a vulnerability is exploited by malware can lead to the development of detection signatures or behavioral indicators for malware identification.

Additionally, it can inform the creation of security patches or mitigations to protect against similar vulnerabilities in legitimate software.

In summary, identifying and exploiting vulnerabilities in malware is a multifaceted and crucial aspect of cybersecurity and malware analysis.

It involves a deep understanding of the malware's code and behavior, as well as ethical considerations and responsible disclosure practices.

The process helps security professionals gain insights into the malware's capabilities, develop countermeasures, and contribute to the overall protection of computer systems and networks.

By effectively identifying and mitigating vulnerabilities in malware, cybersecurity experts play a vital role in defending against cyber threats and ensuring the security of digital environments.

Case studies of vulnerability exploitation provide invaluable insights into real-world security incidents and demonstrate the importance of identifying and mitigating vulnerabilities.

These case studies illustrate how cybercriminals and threat actors leverage vulnerabilities to compromise systems and achieve their malicious objectives.

One notable case study involves the WannaCry ransomware attack in 2017, which exploited a vulnerability in the Windows operating system known as EternalBlue.

The WannaCry ransomware used this vulnerability to propagate rapidly across networks, encrypting files and demanding ransom payments in Bitcoin.

This case highlighted the critical need for organizations to patch their systems promptly to prevent such widespread attacks.

Another significant case study involves the Equifax data breach in 2017, where attackers exploited a known vulnerability in the Apache Struts web application framework.

This breach exposed sensitive personal information of millions of individuals, underscoring the importance of timely patch management and vulnerability assessment.

The Heartbleed vulnerability in the OpenSSL cryptographic library is yet another case study that garnered widespread attention.

This vulnerability allowed attackers to steal sensitive information, including private keys and user data, from vulnerable web servers.

The Heartbleed incident emphasized the importance of promptly updating and patching software to protect against known vulnerabilities.

Additionally, case studies related to software supply chain attacks have gained prominence in recent years.

For example, the SolarWinds supply chain attack in 2020 exploited vulnerabilities in the software supply chain to compromise numerous organizations.

The attackers injected malicious code into legitimate software updates, which were then distributed to unsuspecting customers.

This case study highlighted the need for rigorous supply chain security practices and careful vetting of third-party software components.

Vulnerability exploitation is not limited to the software realm; hardware vulnerabilities can also have significant consequences.

One such case study involves the Meltdown and Spectre vulnerabilities, which affected a wide range of modern microprocessors.

These vulnerabilities allowed attackers to steal sensitive data from the memory of a compromised system, even from isolated applications.

Mitigating these vulnerabilities required a combination of software patches and microcode updates, emphasizing the importance of collaboration between hardware and software vendors.

The Stuxnet worm is a well-known case study of a targeted attack that exploited multiple vulnerabilities to sabotage Iran's nuclear program.

Stuxnet utilized zero-day vulnerabilities, which are previously unknown vulnerabilities that have not been patched.

This case study highlighted the challenges in defending against sophisticated, state-sponsored attacks and the need for robust security measures.

Ransomware attacks have become increasingly prevalent in recent years, with numerous case studies illustrating the devastating impact of these attacks.

The Colonial Pipeline ransomware attack in 2021 disrupted fuel supply across the southeastern United States and underscored the critical infrastructure's vulnerability to cyber threats.

These case studies serve as stark reminders of the importance of robust cybersecurity practices, including regular backups, network segmentation, and user training.

Additionally, the NotPetya ransomware attack in 2017, which initially targeted Ukraine but spread globally, demonstrated the potential for collateral damage resulting from cyberattacks.

NotPetya utilized a vulnerability in accounting software to propagate and encrypt victims' data, causing widespread financial losses.

The case study highlighted the need for organizations to maintain strong incident response plans and disaster recovery capabilities.

Vulnerability exploitation is not limited to external attackers; insiders can also exploit vulnerabilities for various purposes.

The Edward Snowden case is a notable example, where an insider exploited vulnerabilities in the National Security Agency's (NSA) systems to leak classified information.

This case study raised concerns about insider threats and the importance of monitoring and securing internal systems.

Mobile devices are not immune to vulnerability exploitation, as demonstrated by the Pegasus spyware case.

Pegasus, developed by the NSO Group, exploited multiple vulnerabilities in iOS to compromise targeted devices.

This case study emphasized the need for mobile device security and regular updates.

The case studies mentioned above highlight the diverse range of vulnerabilities that threat actors can exploit, including software, hardware, supply chain, and insider vulnerabilities.

They underscore the critical importance of proactive vulnerability management, patching, and ongoing cybersecurity awareness and training.

Organizations must remain vigilant and stay informed about emerging threats to mitigate the risks associated with vulnerability exploitation.

In summary, case studies of vulnerability exploitation provide real-world examples of the impact of cybersecurity vulnerabilities on organizations and individuals.

These incidents underscore the importance of timely patching, supply chain security, and robust cybersecurity practices.

By studying these cases, security professionals can better understand the tactics used by threat actors and develop effective strategies to defend against vulnerabilities.

Chapter 4: Advanced Dynamic Analysis and Debugging

Advanced dynamic analysis tools and setup play a crucial role in the field of cybersecurity and malware analysis.

Dynamic analysis is the process of analyzing malware and suspicious software by executing it in a controlled environment to observe its behavior and interactions with the system.

This approach is essential for gaining insights into the runtime activities of malicious code and understanding its impact on a compromised system.

To perform advanced dynamic analysis, security professionals rely on a variety of specialized tools and carefully configured environments.

One of the fundamental tools for dynamic analysis is the use of virtualization or sandboxing technology.

Virtual machines (VMs) or sandboxes provide isolated and controlled environments where malware can be executed without affecting the host system.

These virtualized environments allow analysts to observe the malware's behavior, monitor its interactions with the operating system, and capture valuable information about its activities.

Advanced dynamic analysis tools often integrate with virtualization technology to provide enhanced monitoring and reporting capabilities.

In addition to virtualization, another crucial component of dynamic analysis is the use of monitoring and instrumentation tools.

These tools capture system-level events, such as file system changes, registry modifications, network traffic, and system calls, while the malware is running.

Advanced monitoring tools offer features like event correlation, behavior analysis, and anomaly detection, enabling analysts to identify suspicious or malicious activities quickly.

Furthermore, dynamic analysis setups involve the use of network capture and analysis tools.

These tools monitor network traffic generated by the malware during execution, providing insights into communication with command and control servers, data exfiltration, and network-based attacks.

Advanced dynamic analysis tools can analyze network traffic patterns, extract payloads, and identify malicious network protocols or patterns.

To set up an effective dynamic analysis environment, analysts must ensure the availability of realistic and representative data.

This includes a variety of malware samples, both known and unknown, to test the dynamic analysis setup thoroughly.

Additionally, analysts may use benign or legitimate software as a baseline for comparison to differentiate normal behavior from malicious activities.

An important consideration in dynamic analysis is the selection of an appropriate host system or environment for running the malware.

The host system should be carefully configured to resemble a typical user or target environment, including the installation of common software and services.

Moreover, analysts often employ techniques like system snapshots and system restore points to revert the host system to a clean state after dynamic analysis, preventing contamination.

Incorporating a wide range of operating systems and configurations into the dynamic analysis setup is essential, as malware may behave differently on various platforms.

For advanced dynamic analysis, analysts may create custom sandbox environments tailored to specific types of malware or threats.

These custom sandboxes can simulate the behavior of specific applications, devices, or environments, providing a deeper understanding of how the malware interacts with its intended targets.

Dynamic analysis often involves the use of automated analysis systems, also known as sandboxes as a service.

These cloud-based platforms allow analysts to submit malware samples for analysis in a remote, controlled environment.

They offer scalability, flexibility, and the ability to analyze multiple samples simultaneously, making them suitable for large-scale analysis efforts.

Advanced dynamic analysis tools and setups should incorporate advanced techniques for code and memory analysis.

These techniques enable analysts to gain a deeper understanding of the malware's inner workings, identify evasion tactics, and uncover vulnerabilities that may be exploited.

Tools for code analysis disassemble and decompile the malware's code, allowing analysts to review its logic, functions, and interactions with system resources.

Memory analysis tools, on the other hand, provide insights into the malware's use of system memory, revealing hidden processes, injected code, and data storage techniques.

Advanced dynamic analysis also includes behavioral analysis, which focuses on identifying malicious behavior patterns exhibited by the malware during execution.

Behavioral analysis tools can detect activities such as file encryption, keylogging, privilege escalation, and attempts to evade detection.

These tools generate comprehensive reports that document the malware's behavior, making it easier for analysts to assess the threat's impact and develop appropriate mitigation strategies.

Another critical aspect of advanced dynamic analysis is the ability to analyze malware families and variants systematically.

Analysts use dynamic analysis results to create behavioral profiles and indicators of compromise (IOCs) that can be used to identify related samples or attacks.

This approach helps security professionals track the evolution of malware and understand the tactics, techniques, and procedures (TTPs) employed by threat actors.

Advanced dynamic analysis setups should incorporate threat intelligence feeds and data correlation to identify links between analyzed samples and known threat actors or campaigns.

Furthermore, integration with incident response processes and security information and event management (SIEM) systems enhances the overall cybersecurity posture of an organization.

To facilitate collaboration and knowledge sharing, dynamic analysis results should be documented comprehensively and stored securely.

These reports serve as valuable references for future analysis, contribute to threat intelligence repositories, and assist in incident response efforts.

Additionally, knowledge sharing within the cybersecurity community helps organizations stay informed about emerging threats and vulnerabilities.

In summary, advanced dynamic analysis tools and setups are essential components of modern cybersecurity practices.

They provide the means to analyze and understand the behavior of malware and other security threats, enabling organizations to develop effective countermeasures and enhance their overall security posture.

By leveraging virtualization, monitoring tools, network analysis, and advanced analysis techniques, security professionals can gain valuable insights into the tactics and strategies employed by threat actors, ultimately strengthening their defense against cyber threats.

Expert debugging strategies are crucial for malware analysts to gain deeper insights into the behavior and inner workings of malicious code.

Debugging is the process of examining and analyzing a program's execution to understand its logic, identify vulnerabilities, and uncover malicious activities.

In the context of malware analysis, debugging is an essential skill that enables analysts to dissect and reverse engineer malicious software effectively.

One of the primary debugging tools used in malware analysis is a debugger, a software application that allows analysts to control the execution of a program, inspect its memory, and track its behavior step by step.

Debuggers provide a dynamic view of the program's execution, enabling analysts to set breakpoints, examine register and memory contents, and follow the flow of execution.

Expert malware analysts are proficient in using a variety of debuggers, including both user-mode and kernel-mode debuggers, to dissect different types of malware.

An essential aspect of expert debugging is setting breakpoints strategically to pause the execution of the malware at specific points of interest.

Analysts may set breakpoints at key function calls, API calls, or critical sections of code to observe the malware's behavior at those points.

By setting breakpoints, analysts can step through the code and monitor the program's state, making it easier to identify malicious activities, such as file manipulation or network communication.

Another advanced debugging technique involves the use of conditional breakpoints, which halt the execution only when certain conditions are met.

This approach is particularly useful for pinpointing specific behaviors or conditions that trigger malicious actions within the malware.

Conditional breakpoints can be set based on memory content, register values, or other runtime conditions, allowing analysts to narrow down their focus during analysis.

In addition to breakpoints, expert malware analysts use watchpoints to track changes to specific memory locations or variables.

Watchpoints notify analysts when a particular memory address is accessed or modified during program execution, helping to identify memory corruption or manipulation by the malware.

To gain a comprehensive understanding of the malware's behavior, analysts may employ multiple debugging sessions in parallel.

By analyzing the same malware sample with different debugging configurations, analysts can cross-reference findings and validate their observations, ensuring accuracy in their analysis.

Expert debugging strategies often involve the use of debugger extensions or plugins that enhance the debugging environment's capabilities.

These extensions can automate certain tasks, provide additional analysis tools, or integrate with specialized tools for code analysis, memory forensics, and network analysis.

For example, the Immunity Debugger, a popular debugger in the malware analysis community, offers various plugins that extend its functionality for analyzing exploits and shellcode.

Additionally, malware analysts are well-versed in utilizing kernel debugging tools for analyzing rootkits and kernel-mode malware.

Kernel debugging allows analysts to inspect and manipulate the operating system's kernel, enabling the analysis of advanced threats that operate at the kernel level.

In-depth knowledge of kernel debugging is essential for understanding the root cause of system compromises and uncovering sophisticated attack techniques.

Expert malware analysts also employ techniques like dynamic taint analysis and data flow tracking during debugging.

Dynamic taint analysis involves marking certain data as "tainted" when it originates from untrusted sources or user input.

By tracking the flow of tainted data within the program, analysts can identify potential vulnerabilities, data leaks, or code injection points exploited by the malware.

Furthermore, advanced debugging strategies involve the use of debug-time patching to modify the malware's behavior during analysis.

Analysts may patch specific instructions, alter register values, or manipulate memory contents to redirect the malware's execution flow or prevent it from performing malicious actions.

Debug-time patching allows analysts to neutralize or bypass certain malware behaviors temporarily, making it safer to analyze the sample.

While debugging, expert malware analysts pay close attention to anti-debugging and anti-analysis techniques employed by the malware.

Malicious software often incorporates evasion tactics to detect and thwart debugging attempts, such as checking for the presence of debuggers or breakpoints.

To counter these techniques, analysts use various methods, including code modification, debugger concealment, and emulation, to deceive the malware into believing it is running in a non-debugged environment.

Furthermore, expert debugging strategies include dynamic analysis of network communications initiated by the malware.

Analysts may intercept and monitor outbound network traffic to identify malicious command and control (C2) communications or data exfiltration attempts.

Network analysis tools, such as Wireshark, are integrated with debugging sessions to capture and analyze network packets generated by the malware.

In cases where malware employs obfuscation or encryption for network communication, analysts may employ dynamic instrumentation to intercept and decrypt the data in real-time.

To facilitate collaboration and knowledge sharing among malware analysts, advanced debugging sessions are meticulously documented.

Comprehensive reports are generated, detailing the malware's behavior, key findings, and indicators of compromise (IOCs).

These reports serve as valuable references for incident response teams, threat intelligence sharing, and future analysis efforts.

In summary, expert debugging strategies are essential for malware analysts to dissect, reverse engineer, and understand the behavior of malicious software effectively.

These strategies involve the use of a variety of debugging tools, breakpoint techniques, conditional breakpoints, watchpoints, and debugger extensions.

Analysts also employ kernel debugging, dynamic taint analysis, and data flow tracking to uncover vulnerabilities and malicious activities.

Debug-time patching, anti-debugging evasion, and network traffic analysis are integral components of advanced debugging sessions.

Overall, expert debugging skills empower malware analysts to unravel the intricacies of malware and contribute to the development of effective mitigation and detection strategies in the ever-evolving landscape of cybersecurity threats.

Chapter 5: Polymorphic and Metamorphic Malware Analysis

Understanding polymorphism and metamorphism is crucial in the field of malware analysis and cybersecurity.

Polymorphism and metamorphism are advanced techniques used by malware authors to evade detection and analysis.

Polymorphic malware is characterized by its ability to change its code or appearance each time it infects a new target.

This dynamic behavior makes it challenging for traditional antivirus solutions to detect and prevent polymorphic malware.

Polymorphic malware achieves its variability through code obfuscation techniques, such as encryption, randomization, and code mutation.

Each time the malware infects a system, it decrypts or generates a unique variant of itself, making it difficult for signature-based detection methods to identify the malware based on static patterns.

The concept of polymorphism draws inspiration from biology, where it refers to the occurrence of multiple forms of an organism within a species.

Similarly, polymorphic malware manifests different forms or instances while retaining its malicious functionality.

Metamorphic malware takes polymorphism to the next level by completely rewriting its code with each infection.

Metamorphic malware not only changes its appearance but also its internal structure and logic.

This metamorphic transformation renders traditional signature-based detection ineffective because there are no consistent patterns or signatures to identify.

Metamorphic malware is akin to a chameleon, constantly adapting and transforming to avoid detection.

To understand polymorphism and metamorphism, malware analysts employ various techniques and tools.

Static analysis involves examining the malware's code without executing it.

During static analysis, analysts aim to identify obfuscation techniques, encryption algorithms, and code mutation routines used by the malware.

This knowledge helps analysts recognize the potential for polymorphic behavior and understand how the malware generates unique variants.

Dynamic analysis, on the other hand, involves executing the malware in a controlled environment to observe its behavior.

During dynamic analysis, analysts can capture the various instances or forms of polymorphic malware as they manifest.

By monitoring the malware's execution and interactions with the system, analysts gain insights into its polymorphic behavior.

Advanced malware analysis tools are equipped with features that assist in identifying and dealing with polymorphic and metamorphic malware.

These tools often include code emulation and runtime analysis capabilities, allowing analysts to observe the malware's behavior in a safe and controlled manner.

Polymorphic and metamorphic malware often employ techniques like self-modifying code, where portions of the code are altered dynamically during execution.

This self-modification makes it challenging to predict the malware's behavior solely from its static code.

To combat polymorphic and metamorphic malware, analysts may utilize heuristic or behavior-based detection methods.

These methods focus on identifying malicious behavior patterns rather than relying on static signatures.

Heuristic analysis involves creating rules and algorithms that flag suspicious behavior, such as code injection, process manipulation, or unauthorized network activity.

Behavior-based detection relies on monitoring the behavior of running processes and alerting on deviations from expected norms.

Behavior-based detection can uncover polymorphic malware by recognizing unusual or malicious actions, even if the malware's code changes.

Pattern recognition is another crucial technique for understanding polymorphism and metamorphism.

Analysts create behavioral patterns or profiles that describe the expected actions of specific types of malware.

These patterns are based on observations made during dynamic analysis and can include sequences of system calls, file operations, and network interactions.

Pattern recognition tools can compare the observed behavior of an analyzed sample to known patterns, helping to identify polymorphic malware variants.

To counter polymorphism and metamorphism, cybersecurity researchers continuously develop and refine detection and analysis techniques.

These efforts include the development of machine learning models capable of recognizing patterns and behaviors associated with polymorphic malware.

Machine learning models can adapt and learn from new samples, making them valuable in the fight against constantly evolving threats.

In addition to automated tools, malware analysts often rely on their expertise and experience in recognizing subtle behavioral anomalies that may indicate polymorphic or metamorphic behavior.

They may use sandboxes and controlled environments to execute malware samples and observe their actions, tracking any deviations from expected behavior.

Sharing knowledge and information within the cybersecurity community is crucial for staying ahead of polymorphic and metamorphic threats.

Collaboration between analysts, researchers, and security practitioners facilitates the exchange of insights and the development of countermeasures.

Furthermore, organizations and security vendors regularly update their threat intelligence feeds and signature databases to incorporate new information about polymorphic and metamorphic malware.

In summary, understanding polymorphism and metamorphism is essential in the field of malware analysis and cybersecurity.

These advanced evasion techniques challenge traditional detection methods, making it imperative for analysts to employ a combination of static and dynamic analysis, heuristic approaches, behavior-based detection, and pattern recognition.

Continuous research and collaboration within the cybersecurity community are vital for developing effective countermeasures against the ever-evolving threat landscape of polymorphic and metamorphic malware.

Analyzing polymorphic and metamorphic malware requires specialized techniques and expertise in the field of cybersecurity and malware analysis.

Polymorphic and metamorphic malware are notorious for their ability to change their code and appearance, making them challenging to detect and analyze.

To effectively analyze polymorphic and metamorphic malware, analysts must employ a combination of static and dynamic analysis methods.

Static analysis involves examining the malware's code without executing it.

During static analysis, analysts scrutinize the code for obfuscation techniques, encryption algorithms, and code mutation routines that are commonly used by polymorphic and metamorphic malware.

These insights help analysts understand the potential for polymorphic behavior and provide clues about how the malware generates unique variants.

Static analysis may also involve disassembling the malware's code, generating an assembly language representation that can be further analyzed for patterns and anomalies.

Furthermore, reverse engineering tools like disassemblers and decompilers can aid in deciphering the malware's logic and structure.

However, static analysis alone may not reveal the full extent of polymorphic and metamorphic behavior.

Dynamic analysis, on the other hand, entails executing the malware in a controlled environment to observe its behavior.

During dynamic analysis, analysts monitor the malware's interactions with the system and capture the various instances or forms it manifests.

This approach is essential for uncovering the true nature of polymorphic and metamorphic malware as it dynamically changes and adapts.

Advanced malware analysis tools equipped with code emulation and runtime analysis capabilities are valuable assets during dynamic analysis.

These tools allow analysts to execute the malware safely and observe its behavior in a controlled environment.

Code emulation mimics the execution of the malware without running it directly on the host system, providing a safe and isolated environment for analysis.

Runtime analysis tools offer real-time monitoring and capture of the malware's activities, helping analysts understand its behavior as it unfolds.

To detect and analyze polymorphic and metamorphic malware, it's essential to identify indicators of compromise (IOCs) that remain consistent across different instances.

This may include identifying common file names, registry keys, or network communication patterns that persist despite the malware's changing code.

Behavior-based detection methods are particularly useful for recognizing these consistent behaviors.

Heuristic analysis involves creating rules and algorithms that flag suspicious behavior, such as code injection, process manipulation, or unauthorized network activity.

By developing heuristics that focus on detecting unusual or malicious actions, analysts can better identify polymorphic and metamorphic malware.

Pattern recognition is another critical technique for understanding and analyzing these elusive threats.

Analysts create behavioral patterns or profiles that describe the expected actions of specific types of malware.

These patterns are based on observations made during dynamic analysis and include sequences of system calls, file operations, and network interactions.

Pattern recognition tools can compare the observed behavior of an analyzed sample to known patterns, helping to identify polymorphic and metamorphic malware variants.

Machine learning models also play a significant role in the analysis of polymorphic and metamorphic malware.

These models can be trained to recognize patterns and behaviors associated with these threats, even as they evolve.

Machine learning can adapt and learn from new samples, making it valuable in the ongoing battle against constantly changing malware.

In addition to automated techniques, malware analysts rely on their expertise and experience to recognize subtle behavioral anomalies that may indicate polymorphic or metamorphic behavior.

They often use sandboxes and controlled environments to execute malware samples and observe their actions while monitoring any deviations from expected behavior.

Collaboration and information sharing within the cybersecurity community are essential for staying ahead of polymorphic and metamorphic threats.

Cybersecurity experts, researchers, and security practitioners must work together to exchange insights and develop effective countermeasures.

Organizations and security vendors regularly update their threat intelligence feeds and signature databases to incorporate new information about polymorphic and metamorphic malware.

In summary, analyzing polymorphic and metamorphic malware demands a multifaceted approach that combines static and dynamic analysis, behavior-based detection, pattern recognition, and machine learning.

These advanced techniques are crucial for understanding and countering the ever-evolving threat landscape posed by polymorphic and metamorphic malware.

Chapter 6: Rootkit Detection and Analysis

Detecting and analyzing malware rootkits is a critical aspect of cybersecurity and malware analysis.

Rootkits are malicious software or tools designed to gain unauthorized access and maintain control over a compromised system.

They often operate at a deep level within an operating system, making them challenging to detect and remove.

Rootkits can be used by attackers to hide their presence, maintain persistence, and conduct various malicious activities on an infected system.

Detecting rootkits requires a combination of advanced techniques and tools specifically designed for rootkit detection.

One common method for detecting rootkits is through the use of integrity-checking tools.

These tools compare the current state of critical system files and configurations to known, trusted versions.

Any discrepancies or changes in these files can indicate the presence of a rootkit.

Integrity-checking tools can help identify unauthorized modifications made by a rootkit to maintain its stealth.

Another technique for rootkit detection involves analyzing system memory and processes.

Rootkits often manipulate system memory to hide their presence or inject malicious code into legitimate processes.

Memory analysis tools can help uncover such anomalies by examining the contents of memory and identifying any unusual or unauthorized activities.

Kernel-level rootkits, which operate at the core of the operating system, are particularly challenging to detect.

They often hook into system calls and manipulate data structures within the kernel.

Rootkit detection tools that operate at the kernel level are necessary to identify these sophisticated threats.

Behavior-based analysis is another approach to rootkit detection.

By monitoring the behavior of running processes and system activities, analysts can identify suspicious or anomalous behavior that may indicate the presence of a rootkit.

This approach focuses on deviations from expected norms and can reveal hidden or stealthy rootkits.

Anti-rootkit tools, specifically designed for detecting and removing rootkits, are available for both Windows and Linux systems.

These tools use a combination of techniques to scan the system for known rootkit signatures, patterns, and behaviors.

They can also conduct memory and file system checks to identify rootkit artifacts and inconsistencies.

Analyzing rootkits often involves reverse engineering and examining the rootkit's code or components.

Rootkit code can be complex and well-hidden, making it challenging to understand and dissect.

Reverse engineering tools, such as disassemblers and decompilers, assist analysts in understanding the inner workings of the rootkit.

Furthermore, experts may use sandboxing environments to execute the rootkit in a controlled setting for behavioral analysis.

Rootkits may employ various evasion techniques to avoid detection.

They can hide their files and processes, modify system logs, and use root-level privileges to conceal their activities.

Rootkit analysis must include checking for hidden files, registry entries, and malicious hooks within the operating system.

Rootkit removal is a delicate process that requires caution to avoid damaging the compromised system.

Anti-rootkit tools are specifically designed for removing rootkits, but their effectiveness depends on the complexity and sophistication of the rootkit.

In some cases, a complete system reinstallation may be necessary to ensure the removal of all rootkit components.

Rootkit analysis also involves understanding the rootkit's purpose and capabilities.

Some rootkits are designed for espionage, data theft, or remote control of infected systems.

Others may focus on maintaining persistence and providing backdoor access to attackers.

Understanding the rootkit's objectives is essential for determining the potential impact on the compromised system and the data it stores.

Rootkits can be used as part of a larger attack campaign, so uncovering their presence is crucial for comprehensive threat mitigation.

Additionally, organizations must implement proactive security measures to prevent rootkit infections in the first place.

This includes keeping operating systems and software up to date, employing strong access controls, and regularly monitoring system activity for signs of compromise.

Security awareness and training for end-users can also help prevent the inadvertent installation of rootkits through social engineering attacks.

Rootkit analysis is an ongoing process, as new rootkit variants and evasion techniques continue to emerge.

Collaboration within the cybersecurity community and sharing of threat intelligence are essential for staying informed about the latest rootkit threats and developing effective countermeasures.

In summary, detecting and analyzing malware rootkits is a critical component of cybersecurity and malware analysis.

It requires a combination of advanced techniques, tools, and expertise to uncover these stealthy and malicious threats.

Rootkits can have serious implications for system security and data integrity, making their detection and removal a top priority for organizations and security professionals.

Continuous research and collaboration are essential to stay ahead of evolving rootkit threats and develop effective defense strategies.

Advanced rootkit detection techniques are crucial for identifying and mitigating the sophisticated and stealthy threats that can compromise system integrity.

Traditional antivirus software and signature-based detection methods are often ineffective against rootkits due to their ability to hide within the operating system.

One advanced technique for rootkit detection involves analyzing system memory for anomalies and inconsistencies.

Rootkits often manipulate system memory to hide their presence, and memory analysis can reveal hidden processes, hooks, and malicious code injections.

Memory forensics tools, such as Volatility and Rekall, are invaluable for conducting this type of analysis.

Another advanced approach to rootkit detection is the use of behavior-based anomaly detection.

By monitoring the behavior of processes and system activities, security analysts can identify deviations from expected norms that may indicate the presence of a rootkit.

This approach focuses on identifying suspicious or unusual behavior rather than relying on known signatures.

Machine learning algorithms can play a significant role in behavior-based rootkit detection.

These algorithms can be trained to recognize patterns and behaviors associated with rootkit activity, even as rootkits evolve and adapt.

Heuristic analysis, a form of behavior-based detection, involves creating rules and algorithms that flag behavior consistent with rootkit activity.

Heuristics are particularly useful for identifying previously unknown rootkits.

Kernel-level rootkits, which operate at the core of the operating system, are some of the most challenging to detect.

They often manipulate system calls and data structures within the kernel, making them highly stealthy.

Advanced rootkit detection tools must operate at the kernel level to identify these sophisticated threats.

Rootkit detection tools can employ techniques such as system call hooking detection, driver signature validation, and direct kernel object manipulation detection.

System call hooking detection identifies alterations made by rootkits to system call tables, which can be a sign of malicious activity.

Driver signature validation ensures that all kernel-mode drivers are properly signed, which can help detect unauthorized driver installations.

Direct kernel object manipulation detection checks for any unauthorized modifications to critical kernel objects.

Rootkit detection tools also benefit from utilizing hardware-assisted virtualization technology to create isolated environments for analysis.

These environments, known as sandboxes, allow analysts to execute suspicious code safely and observe its behavior without risking the integrity of the host system.

Sandboxing is particularly useful for rootkit analysis as it prevents the rootkit from detecting the analysis environment and evading detection.

Rootkit detection tools can also utilize hardware-based features such as Intel VT-x and AMD-V to isolate and analyze potentially malicious code.

Network traffic analysis is another advanced technique for rootkit detection.

Some rootkits establish covert communication channels to command and control servers, allowing attackers to remotely control compromised systems.

By monitoring network traffic for unusual patterns or connections to known malicious domains or IP addresses, analysts can detect rootkit-related network activity.

Network intrusion detection systems (NIDS) and network packet analyzers can be valuable tools for this type of analysis.

Advanced rootkit detection often involves the use of specialized anti-rootkit software designed to identify and remove rootkits from infected systems.

These tools employ a combination of the techniques mentioned earlier, including memory analysis, behavior-based anomaly detection, and kernel-level checks.

Rootkit detection software can be used proactively to scan systems for signs of rootkit infections or reactively to investigate suspicious activity.

However, it's important to note that rootkit detection tools must be regularly updated to stay effective against evolving rootkit threats.

In addition to using advanced detection techniques, organizations should implement proactive security measures to prevent rootkit infections.

This includes regularly patching and updating operating systems and software, employing strong access controls, and educating users about the risks of downloading and executing untrusted files.

Regularly monitoring system activity and performing periodic security assessments can also help detect rootkit infections early.

Collaboration and information sharing within the cybersecurity community are essential for staying informed about the latest rootkit threats and developing effective countermeasures.

In summary, advanced rootkit detection techniques are essential for identifying and mitigating the complex and stealthy threats that rootkits pose to system security.

These techniques encompass memory analysis, behavior-based anomaly detection, kernel-level checks, sandboxing, network traffic analysis, and specialized anti-rootkit software.

Proactive security measures and continuous research and collaboration within the cybersecurity community are crucial for staying ahead of evolving rootkit threats and defending against them effectively.

Chapter 7: Malware Behavior Analysis and Reverse Engineering

In-depth behavior analysis of malware is a crucial step in understanding the impact and potential risks posed by malicious software.

It involves a comprehensive examination of how malware behaves within a compromised system and the actions it takes to achieve its objectives.

Behavior analysis is an essential component of malware analysis and is particularly valuable for identifying previously unknown threats.

Behavior analysis begins by executing the malware in a controlled and isolated environment known as a sandbox.

The sandbox allows security analysts to observe the malware's actions without risking the integrity of the host system.

During execution, the behavior of the malware is closely monitored, and all system interactions, network communications, file modifications, and registry changes are recorded.

Behavior analysis aims to answer several key questions about the malware's actions and intentions.

One critical question is, "What is the malware's primary objective?"

Understanding the malware's goal is essential for assessing the potential impact on the compromised system and the data it contains.

Some malware is designed for data theft, while others focus on maintaining persistence or providing remote access to attackers.

Behavior analysis helps uncover the malware's intended purpose.

Another crucial question is, "How does the malware achieve its objectives?"

Malware often employs a variety of techniques to achieve its goals, including file manipulation, registry modifications, process injection, and network communication.

Analyzing these techniques provides insights into the malware's tactics and capabilities.

Behavior analysis also helps answer the question, "What is the malware's evasion strategy?"

Many malware variants incorporate evasion techniques to avoid detection and analysis.

These techniques can include anti-analysis checks, obfuscation, and attempts to hide their presence.

Identifying these evasion tactics is essential for developing effective countermeasures.

Behavior analysis extends to understanding the malware's propagation methods.

Some malware spreads through email attachments, while others exploit vulnerabilities or use social engineering tactics.

Analyzing how the malware spreads can help organizations strengthen their defenses against infection.

In-depth behavior analysis also includes examining the malware's interaction with the compromised system's resources.

This involves monitoring its use of system resources such as CPU, memory, and disk space.

Malware can consume significant system resources, leading to system slowdowns or crashes.

Understanding how the malware impacts resource utilization is essential for assessing its operational impact.

Behavior analysis provides insights into the malware's persistence mechanisms.

Malware often employs techniques to ensure it remains on the compromised system even after a system reboot.

Analyzing these persistence mechanisms helps security analysts identify how to remove the malware effectively.

Furthermore, behavior analysis reveals the malware's communication patterns.

Malware often establishes communication channels with command and control servers operated by attackers.

These channels allow attackers to remotely control compromised systems.

Understanding the communication protocols and destinations is crucial for blocking malicious network traffic.

Behavior analysis also involves monitoring any modifications made to system settings or configurations by the malware.

Malware may alter firewall rules, disable security software, or change registry keys to maintain control over the compromised system.

Identifying these changes is essential for restoring the system to a secure state.

Behavior analysis often involves dynamic analysis, where the malware is executed in a controlled environment to observe its actions in real-time.

Static analysis, on the other hand, examines the malware's code and file structures without execution.

Combining both dynamic and static analysis techniques provides a comprehensive view of the malware's behavior.

Behavior analysis can be automated using various sandboxing and analysis tools.

These tools can generate detailed reports that document the malware's actions, interactions, and system modifications.

Security analysts rely on these reports to make informed decisions about the severity of the malware infection and develop appropriate response strategies.

Behavior analysis is a continuous process, as malware constantly evolves to evade detection and analysis.

Collaboration within the cybersecurity community and the sharing of threat intelligence play a vital role in staying ahead of emerging threats.

In summary, in-depth behavior analysis of malware is a critical aspect of cybersecurity and malware analysis.

It involves a comprehensive examination of how malware behaves within a compromised system, including its objectives, tactics, evasion strategies, propagation methods, resource utilization, persistence mechanisms, communication patterns, and system modifications.

Behavior analysis helps security professionals understand the full scope of a malware infection and develop effective mitigation and response strategies to protect against evolving threats. Reverse engineering malware behavior patterns is a fundamental process in understanding the actions and intentions of malicious software.

It involves a systematic analysis of how malware behaves within an infected system, helping security professionals identify its objectives and potential risks.

Malware behavior patterns provide valuable insights into the malware's functionality and tactics, aiding in the development of effective countermeasures.

The first step in reverse engineering malware behavior patterns is to obtain a sample of the malicious software.

This sample can be obtained through various means, such as network traffic capture, email attachments, or file downloads. Once the malware sample is acquired, it is essential to create a controlled and isolated environment for analysis.

This environment, often referred to as a sandbox, allows security analysts to execute the malware safely and observe its behavior without compromising the integrity of the host system.

Behavior analysis of malware involves monitoring the actions the malware takes upon execution.

These actions can include file system modifications, registry changes, process creation, and network communication.

Security analysts record and analyze each action to build a comprehensive understanding of the malware's behavior.

One crucial aspect of reverse engineering malware behavior patterns is determining the malware's primary objective.

Understanding what the malware aims to achieve is essential for assessing the potential impact on the infected system and any data it may compromise.

Some malware is designed for data theft, while others focus on maintaining persistence or providing remote access to attackers.

Analyzing the malware's behavior helps uncover its intended purpose.

Behavior analysis also aims to answer the question, "How does the malware achieve its objectives?"

Malware often employs a variety of techniques to achieve its goals, including exploiting vulnerabilities, propagating through network shares, and executing code injection.

Analyzing these techniques provides insights into the malware's tactics and capabilities.

In addition to understanding the malware's goals and tactics, behavior analysis seeks to uncover the malware's evasion strategies.

Many malware variants incorporate evasion techniques to avoid detection and analysis.

These techniques can include anti-analysis checks, obfuscation, and attempts to hide their presence.

Identifying these evasion tactics is crucial for developing effective countermeasures. Behavior analysis extends to examining the malware's propagation methods.

Some malware spreads through email attachments, while others exploit vulnerabilities or use social engineering tactics. Analyzing how the malware spreads can help organizations strengthen their defenses against infection.

In-depth behavior analysis also includes monitoring the malware's interaction with the compromised system's resources. This involves tracking its use of system resources such as CPU, memory, and disk space.

Malware can consume significant system resources, leading to system slowdowns or crashes.

Understanding how the malware impacts resource utilization is essential for assessing its operational impact.

Behavior analysis provides insights into the malware's persistence mechanisms.

Malware often employs techniques to ensure it remains on the compromised system even after a system reboot.

Analyzing these persistence mechanisms helps security analysts identify how to remove the malware effectively.

Furthermore, behavior analysis reveals the malware's communication patterns.

Malware often establishes communication channels with command and control servers operated by attackers.

These channels allow attackers to remotely control compromised systems.

Understanding the communication protocols and destinations is crucial for blocking malicious network traffic.

Behavior analysis also involves monitoring any modifications made to system settings or configurations by the malware.

Malware may alter firewall rules, disable security software, or change registry keys to maintain control over the compromised system.

Identifying these changes is essential for restoring the system to a secure state.

Behavior analysis often involves dynamic analysis, where the malware is executed in a controlled environment to observe its actions in real-time.

Static analysis, on the other hand, examines the malware's code and file structures without execution.

Combining both dynamic and static analysis techniques provides a comprehensive view of the malware's behavior.

Behavior analysis can be automated using various sandboxing and analysis tools.

These tools can generate detailed reports that document the malware's actions, interactions, and system modifications.

Security analysts rely on these reports to make informed decisions about the severity of the malware infection and develop appropriate response strategies.

Behavior analysis is a continuous process, as malware constantly evolves to evade detection and analysis.

Collaboration within the cybersecurity community and the sharing of threat intelligence play a vital role in staying ahead of emerging threats.

In summary, reverse engineering malware behavior patterns is a critical aspect of cybersecurity and malware analysis.

It involves a comprehensive examination of how malware behaves within an infected system, including its objectives, tactics, evasion strategies, propagation methods, resource utilization, persistence mechanisms, communication patterns, and system modifications.

Behavior analysis helps security professionals understand the full scope of a malware infection and develop effective mitigation and response strategies to protect against evolving threats.

Chapter 8: Malware Reverse Engineering for Forensics

Malware analysis plays a crucial role in digital forensics, aiding investigators in uncovering the source, impact, and scope of malicious activities in digital environments.

Digital forensics aims to collect, preserve, analyze, and present digital evidence in legal proceedings or cybersecurity incident response.

Malware analysis is an integral component of this process, as it helps identify and understand malicious software's behavior and potential implications.

One of the primary objectives of malware analysis in digital forensics is to determine how and when the malware entered the compromised system.

By analyzing the malware's artifacts, timestamps, and indicators of compromise, investigators can reconstruct the timeline of the attack and the initial infection vector.

Understanding the entry point is essential for identifying potential vulnerabilities or attack vectors that need mitigation.

Malware analysis also assists in assessing the malware's persistence mechanisms, which enable it to maintain control over the compromised system.

These mechanisms may include the creation of malicious registry entries, scheduled tasks, or rogue services.

Identifying and documenting these persistence techniques is vital for eliminating the malware and securing the affected system.

Furthermore, malware analysis helps investigators examine the malware's propagation methods within a network.

Understanding how the malware spreads or communicates with other systems is crucial for containing the infection and preventing further compromise.

Malware may use various techniques, such as exploiting vulnerabilities, propagating through email attachments, or leveraging lateral movement within a network.

Analyzing these propagation mechanisms helps trace the malware's path and the extent of its reach. Digital forensics professionals also rely on malware analysis to determine the malware's intended objectives. Some malware is designed for data theft, while others focus on providing attackers with remote control over compromised systems.

Identifying the malware's goals is essential for assessing the potential impact on sensitive data and intellectual property.

Malware analysis also helps uncover valuable information about the attackers behind the malicious software.

Examining the malware's code, network communications, and infrastructure connections can provide insights into the threat actor's identity, motives, and techniques.

Attribution, while challenging, can be critical for legal proceedings and future cybersecurity strategies.

In digital forensics, malware analysis assists in collecting evidence related to the malware infection and its impact on digital assets.

This evidence can be used in court to support criminal or civil cases and is subject to strict chain-of-custody protocols to maintain its integrity.

Digital forensics professionals employ a variety of tools and techniques for malware analysis.

Dynamic analysis involves executing the malware in a controlled environment, often referred to as a sandbox, to observe its behavior in real-time.

This approach allows investigators to monitor the malware's actions, including file modifications, registry changes, and network communications.

Static analysis, on the other hand, involves examining the malware's code and file structure without execution.

This technique helps identify malicious signatures, patterns, and indicators of compromise.

Combining dynamic and static analysis provides a comprehensive view of the malware's behavior and characteristics.

Memory analysis is another critical aspect of malware analysis in digital forensics.

Investigators examine the system's memory for signs of malicious activity, such as injected code, rootkits, or hidden processes.

Memory forensics can uncover stealthy malware that traditional disk-based analysis may miss.

Malware analysis in digital forensics also encompasses reverse engineering, a process that involves dissecting the malware's code to understand its inner workings.

Reverse engineering helps investigators identify vulnerabilities, exploits, and potential countermeasures.

Additionally, malware analysis includes the examination of network traffic to identify communication patterns and detect malicious command and control connections.

Analyzing network traffic helps trace back to the source of the malware and the infrastructure used by threat actors.

In digital forensics, documenting findings is of paramount importance.

Investigators create detailed reports that outline the malware's behavior, propagation methods, impact, and indicators of compromise.

These reports serve as crucial documentation for legal proceedings and incident response efforts.

In summary, malware analysis plays a vital role in digital forensics by helping investigators understand the source, behavior, and impact of malicious software in digital environments.

It aids in determining the entry point of the malware, its persistence mechanisms, propagation methods, intended objectives, and potential attribution.

Malware analysis encompasses dynamic and static analysis, memory forensics, reverse engineering, and network traffic analysis, all aimed at providing a comprehensive view of the malware's behavior and characteristics.

The findings from malware analysis are documented in detailed reports, which are essential for legal proceedings and incident response efforts, ultimately aiding in maintaining the integrity of digital environments and supporting cybersecurity investigations.

Leveraging malware analysis in forensic investigations is a critical and multifaceted process that assists digital forensic professionals in uncovering the intricacies of cybercrimes.

Digital forensics involves the collection, preservation, analysis, and presentation of digital evidence, and malware analysis is an indispensable component of this endeavor.

One primary objective of integrating malware analysis into forensic investigations is to identify the nature and behavior of malicious software encountered during an incident.

This includes understanding how the malware infiltrated the compromised system, whether through a phishing email, a software vulnerability, or another vector of attack.

By dissecting the malware's entry point, forensic analysts can establish a comprehensive timeline of the breach, crucial for reconstructing the sequence of events leading up to the incident.

Malware analysis also helps in ascertaining the malware's persistence mechanisms, which are crucial for maintaining control over the compromised system.

These mechanisms may involve the creation of registry keys, scheduled tasks, or rogue services that ensure the malware persists even after system reboots.

Identifying and documenting these persistence techniques is pivotal for effective malware removal and system remediation.

Moreover, malware analysis aids forensic investigators in unraveling the malware's propagation methods, allowing them to trace the path the malware took within a network.

This is essential for understanding the extent of the infection and preventing its further spread.

Malware can use a variety of tactics to propagate, such as exploiting vulnerabilities, utilizing malicious email attachments, or engaging in lateral movement within the network.

Analyzing these propagation mechanisms is indispensable for tracking the malware's reach and devising containment strategies.

Understanding the malware's objectives is another critical facet of malware analysis in forensic investigations.

By discerning whether the malware is designed for data exfiltration, surveillance, disruption, or any other purpose, investigators can gauge its potential impact and the risks posed to the affected organization.

Malware analysis is a valuable tool for uncovering the attackers behind the malicious software.

Examining the malware's code, network communications, and infrastructure connections can provide insights into the threat actor's identity, motivations, and tactics.

Attribution, though challenging, can be pivotal for legal proceedings and for organizations to enhance their security posture.

In the realm of digital forensics, malware analysis is instrumental in collecting evidence related to the malware infection and its impact on digital assets.

This evidence is crucial for supporting criminal or civil cases, and it is subject to stringent chain-of-custody procedures to preserve its integrity.

The field of malware analysis employs a diverse range of tools and techniques, each serving a specific purpose.

Dynamic analysis entails the execution of malware within a controlled environment, commonly referred to as a sandbox, to monitor its real-time behavior.

This approach allows investigators to observe the malware's actions, such as file modifications, registry changes, and network communications.

Static analysis, conversely, involves scrutinizing the malware's code and file structure without executing it.

This method is particularly useful for identifying malicious signatures, patterns, and indicators of compromise.

The combination of dynamic and static analysis provides a comprehensive understanding of the malware's behavior and characteristics.

Memory analysis is a pivotal aspect of malware analysis in digital forensics.

Forensic experts scrutinize the system's memory for signs of malicious activity, such as injected code, rootkits, or hidden processes.

Memory forensics can reveal stealthy malware that traditional disk-based analysis may overlook.

Reverse engineering is another indispensable technique in malware analysis, involving the dissection of the malware's code to comprehend its inner workings.

Reverse engineering assists investigators in identifying vulnerabilities, exploits, and potential mitigation measures.

Furthermore, malware analysis encompasses the examination of network traffic to detect communication patterns and malicious command and control connections.

This aids in tracing the malware back to its source and the infrastructure used by threat actors.

In the context of digital forensics, meticulous documentation is of utmost importance.

Investigators generate detailed reports that encompass the malware's behavior, propagation methods, impact, and indicators of compromise.

These reports serve as vital documentation for legal proceedings and incident response efforts, aiding in preserving the integrity of digital environments and supporting cybersecurity investigations.

To sum up, malware analysis plays a pivotal role in digital forensic investigations by enabling professionals to unravel the complexities of cybercrimes.

It assists in understanding the malware's entry point, persistence mechanisms, propagation methods, intended objectives, and potential attribution.

Malware analysis encompasses dynamic and static analysis, memory forensics, reverse engineering, and network traffic analysis, all of which contribute to a comprehensive view of the malware's behavior.

The findings from malware analysis are meticulously documented in reports that are indispensable for legal proceedings and incident response efforts, ultimately contributing to the preservation of digital environments and the successful resolution of cybersecurity incidents.

Chapter 9: Advanced Anti-Reverse Engineering Techniques

In the ever-evolving landscape of cybersecurity, threat actors are constantly devising new and innovative ways to protect their malicious code from reverse engineering attempts.

To overcome these anti-reverse engineering measures, analysts and researchers must employ advanced techniques and strategies. One of the most common anti-reverse engineering techniques employed by malware authors is code obfuscation. Code obfuscation involves intentionally adding complexity to the codebase, making it challenging for analysts to understand the program's logic and functions.

To tackle obfuscated code, reverse engineers often employ deobfuscation tools and techniques that aim to simplify and clarify the code. These tools can help reveal the underlying functionality of the malware and make it more accessible for analysis. Another effective anti-reverse engineering measure is the use of packers and crypters, which encrypt or compress the malware's executable file.

When the malware is executed, it dynamically unpacks itself in memory, making it difficult to analyze the original code stored on disk. To address this, analysts can employ memory analysis techniques to inspect the unpacked code while it resides in the system's memory. Dynamic analysis tools, such as debuggers and disassemblers, are essential for examining malware in its unpacked state. Polymorphic and metamorphic malware pose additional challenges for reverse engineers. Polymorphic malware changes its appearance each time it infects a new system, making signature-based detection ineffective.

Metamorphic malware goes a step further by actively altering its code each time it executes, making it extremely difficult to analyze.

To combat these forms of malware, researchers have developed specialized tools and heuristics that can identify and classify patterns within the code.

These tools aim to recognize common functions or behavior, allowing analysts to understand the malware's core functionality.

Rootkit-based malware represents another layer of complexity in the battle against anti-reverse engineering measures.

Rootkits are designed to conceal their presence on a compromised system by altering system components and intercepting system calls.

To uncover rootkits, analysts must employ techniques such as memory forensics and kernel-level debugging.

These methods enable the examination of the kernel's memory and system structures to identify irregularities and hidden processes.

Another challenging anti-reverse engineering measure is the use of anti-debugging and anti-analysis tricks within the malware.

Malware authors often implement checks to detect if their code is running within a debugger or analysis environment.

To counter these anti-debugging measures, reverse engineers can utilize debugging tools that employ stealthy debugging techniques to avoid detection.

These tools allow analysts to manipulate the execution flow of the malware without triggering anti-analysis mechanisms.

Network communication is a crucial aspect of malware analysis, and some advanced malware strains employ encryption and secure protocols to hide their malicious activities.

Reverse engineers must employ techniques for decrypting and inspecting encrypted network traffic to understand the malware's communication patterns.

Moreover, malware may employ evasion techniques to avoid detection by security software, such as sandboxing and virtual machine detection.

To address this, analysts can set up customized analysis environments that mimic real-world conditions and avoid triggering the malware's evasion mechanisms.

In some cases, malware may employ steganography to hide data within seemingly innocuous files or images. To detect and extract hidden information, analysts can use specialized steganalysis tools and techniques.

Additionally, some malware strains use advanced anti-reverse engineering measures like self-modifying code, which dynamically alters its instructions during execution.

To analyze such malware, reverse engineers must use tools that can track and analyze code changes as they occur in real-time.

Furthermore, anti-reverse engineering measures may include anti-sandboxing and anti-emulation techniques that aim to identify the analysis environment.

To counter these measures, analysts can implement custom sandboxing and emulation environments that mimic legitimate systems and avoid triggering anti-analysis checks.

In summary, dealing with advanced anti-reverse engineering measures requires a combination of specialized tools, techniques, and expertise.

Analysts must be prepared to tackle code obfuscation, packers, polymorphic and metamorphic malware, rootkits, anti-debugging tricks, and encrypted network communication.

Customized analysis environments and the use of stealthy debugging techniques are essential for bypassing evasion mechanisms and anti-analysis tricks. Moreover, steganalysis and tracking self-modifying code are crucial for uncovering hidden information and analyzing dynamic malware.

Overcoming obfuscation and evasion techniques is a fundamental challenge in the field of cybersecurity and malware analysis. Malware authors employ these strategies to make their malicious code difficult to detect and analyze, requiring advanced methods and tools to decipher their intentions. Obfuscation techniques involve intentionally adding complexity to the code to hinder reverse engineers' efforts in understanding the malware's functionality.

One common obfuscation method is the use of meaningless variable and function names, making it challenging to discern the purpose of different code segments.

To counter obfuscation, reverse engineers employ deobfuscation tools and manual analysis to simplify and clarify the code.

These tools aim to rename variables and functions, making the code more readable and revealing the underlying functionality.

Another obfuscation technique is control flow obfuscation, where the malware author rearranges the order of instructions to create convoluted control flow paths.

This makes it challenging to follow the logical flow of the program.

To tackle control flow obfuscation, analysts use control flow analysis tools and control flow graph reconstruction techniques to identify the true execution path and understand the code's logic.

String encryption is another common obfuscation technique where the malware encrypts strings containing critical information, such as URLs or command and control server addresses.

This makes it difficult to identify the malicious network communication.

Reverse engineers must employ techniques to decrypt and extract these hidden strings, allowing them to uncover the malware's communication patterns.

Moreover, some malware employs runtime packers or crypters, which encrypt or compress the executable code.

The malware then dynamically unpacks itself in memory during execution, complicating the analysis process.

To address this, analysts use memory analysis techniques to inspect the unpacked code while it resides in the system's memory.

Dynamic analysis tools like debuggers and disassemblers are crucial for examining malware in its unpacked state.

To further obscure their intentions, malware authors use evasion techniques to avoid detection by security software and analysis environments.

Anti-debugging and anti-analysis tricks are often implemented to detect if the code is running within a debugger or virtual machine.

Reverse engineers must employ stealthy debugging techniques to manipulate the execution flow of the malware without triggering these anti-analysis mechanisms.

Network communication is a vital aspect of malware analysis, but some advanced malware strains use encryption and secure protocols to hide their activities.

Analysts must employ techniques for decrypting and inspecting encrypted network traffic to understand the malware's communication patterns fully.

Additionally, malware may employ evasion techniques to avoid detection by security software, such as sandboxing and virtual machine detection.

To counter these measures, analysts can set up customized analysis environments that mimic real-world conditions and avoid triggering the malware's evasion mechanisms. In some cases, malware may employ steganography to hide data within seemingly innocuous files or images.

To detect and extract hidden information, analysts can use specialized steganalysis tools and techniques. Furthermore, some malware strains use self-modifying code, which dynamically alters its instructions during execution. To analyze such malware, reverse engineers must use tools that can track and analyze code changes in real-time. Moreover, anti-reverse engineering measures may include anti-sandboxing and anti-emulation techniques that aim to identify the analysis environment.

To counter these measures, analysts can implement custom sandboxing and emulation environments that mimic legitimate systems and avoid triggering anti-analysis checks.

In summary, overcoming obfuscation and evasion techniques in malware analysis is a complex and ever-evolving challenge.

Malware authors employ these strategies to make their code unreadable and to avoid detection by security solutions.

Reverse engineers must continuously adapt their skills and utilize advanced tools to decipher the true intentions of the malware.

Deobfuscation, control flow analysis, string decryption, memory analysis, stealthy debugging, and steganalysis are all crucial techniques in the battle against obfuscation and evasion.

By staying informed about the latest threats and continually developing their expertise, analysts can effectively overcome these challenges and protect digital environments from sophisticated malware.

Chapter 10: Expert-Level Case Studies in Malware Analysis

In-depth analysis of complex malware samples represents a significant milestone in the field of cybersecurity and threat intelligence.

Complex malware is designed to be highly sophisticated, evasive, and challenging to detect, making it a prime target for in-depth analysis.

Such malware often possesses advanced capabilities, including rootkit functionalities, polymorphic code, and encryption techniques, which require meticulous examination.

The first step in analyzing complex malware involves obtaining a reliable sample for analysis, typically from a compromised system or a controlled environment.

Once obtained, the malware sample must be safely contained within an isolated and controlled environment to prevent unintended consequences, such as spreading to other systems.

Isolating the sample is crucial to protect the analyst's system and network from potential harm.

Next, analysts proceed to perform static analysis of the malware, examining its code and components without executing it.

During static analysis, researchers extract valuable information about the malware, including file properties, metadata, and embedded resources.

They also identify any known signatures, patterns, or indicators of compromise (IOCs) within the sample.

Additionally, analysts use static analysis to dissect the malware's structure, reverse engineer its assembly code, and uncover its internal logic.

This process often reveals the malware's functionality, its potential attack vectors, and the techniques it employs to evade detection.

In-depth static analysis may also uncover the presence of code obfuscation or packing, which further complicates the analysis.

Code obfuscation is a common technique used by malware authors to obscure the purpose and functionality of their code.

Reverse engineers must deobfuscate the code to make it more intelligible and reveal its true intent. Similarly, packed malware requires dynamic analysis to unpack and analyze the executable code, as executing it within the packed state may not provide a clear understanding of its functionality.

Dynamic analysis involves running the malware in a controlled and monitored environment to observe its behavior and interactions with the host system.

Researchers employ various dynamic analysis techniques, including sandboxing, emulating different operating systems, and monitoring system calls and network traffic.

Through dynamic analysis, analysts can capture critical information about the malware's execution flow, such as its entry points, system interactions, and file system modifications.

Furthermore, dynamic analysis helps uncover the malware's evasion tactics, such as anti-debugging techniques and attempts to detect analysis environments.

Advanced malware often employs rootkit functionalities to gain persistence and stealthily maintain control over the compromised system.

Rootkits operate at the kernel level, making them difficult to detect and analyze.

To analyze rootkit-based malware, researchers must employ specialized techniques like memory forensics and kernel debugging.

Memory forensics allows analysts to inspect the contents of the system's physical memory, revealing hidden processes, altered system structures, and potential rootkit artifacts.

Kernel debugging tools and techniques enable researchers to interact with the kernel, tracing system calls, and identifying anomalies or hooking points where rootkits may be operating.

Additionally, complex malware samples may exhibit polymorphic or metamorphic behavior, which further complicates analysis.

Polymorphic malware generates different code variants with each infection, making signature-based detection ineffective.

Metamorphic malware goes even further, actively changing its code during execution to thwart analysis.

To analyze such malware, researchers must develop custom tools or employ advanced heuristic and machine learning techniques to identify behavioral patterns and classify variants.

Complex malware may also employ evasion mechanisms to avoid detection by security solutions, including anti-virtualization, anti-sandboxing, and anti-analysis techniques.

Analysts must be aware of these evasion tactics and employ countermeasures to prevent the malware from detecting and escaping the analysis environment.

Furthermore, analysis of complex malware samples often requires collaboration among cybersecurity experts with diverse skill sets, including reverse engineering, network forensics, and threat intelligence.

Through collaboration, researchers can combine their expertise to gain a comprehensive understanding of the malware's capabilities and intent.

In summary, conducting in-depth analysis of complex malware samples is a critical endeavor in the realm of cybersecurity.

Such malware poses significant threats to organizations and individuals alike, and understanding its inner workings is essential for effective defense and mitigation.

In-depth analysis involves both static and dynamic analysis, code deobfuscation, rootkit detection, and the identification of evasion techniques.

It requires a combination of specialized tools, techniques, and interdisciplinary collaboration to unravel the complexity and sophistication of these malicious programs.

By mastering these analytical approaches, cybersecurity professionals can better protect digital environments and respond effectively to emerging threats.

Expert insights from real-world malware analysis cases provide invaluable knowledge and lessons for cybersecurity professionals.

These insights offer a glimpse into the constantly evolving tactics, techniques, and procedures (TTPs) employed by malicious actors in the digital landscape.

By examining these cases, analysts can enhance their understanding of emerging threats and improve their ability to defend against them.

Real-world malware analysis cases often involve sophisticated attacks targeting various sectors, including government agencies, corporations, and critical infrastructure.

These cases highlight the significance of thorough and timely analysis to detect and mitigate threats effectively.

In many instances, malware samples are collected from compromised systems or incident response investigations.

These samples serve as the foundation for detailed analysis and offer a firsthand look at the malicious code's inner workings.

Malware analysts work diligently to deconstruct the malware, uncover its functionalities, and identify its objectives.

One common objective is data exfiltration, where malware attempts to steal sensitive information, such as login credentials or confidential documents.

Analysts examine the malware's data exfiltration techniques, which may involve the use of covert channels or encrypted communication to avoid detection.

Another prevalent objective of malware is to establish persistence within the compromised system.

Malicious actors aim to ensure their presence remains undetected for as long as possible.

To achieve this, they employ various techniques, such as modifying the Windows Registry, creating hidden files, or exploiting vulnerabilities in the operating system.

Through the analysis of real-world cases, experts gain insights into these persistence mechanisms and develop countermeasures to detect and remove persistent threats.

In some cases, malware exhibits self-propagation capabilities, enabling it to spread across networks and infect multiple systems.

Worms and botnets are examples of malware types designed to propagate and form a network of compromised devices under the control of malicious actors.

Malware analysts examine the propagation techniques employed by these threats, such as exploiting software vulnerabilities, brute-forcing weak passwords, or using social engineering tactics.

They also study the command and control infrastructure used by botnets to communicate with and control compromised devices. By understanding these mechanisms, experts can disrupt botnets and prevent further infections. Real-world malware analysis often reveals the use of evasion techniques to avoid detection by security solutions. These techniques include code obfuscation, anti-virtualization measures, and the use of rootkit functionalities.

Analysts delve into these evasion tactics to identify ways to circumvent them and improve detection capabilities.

Advanced malware strains may incorporate sandbox detection mechanisms, allowing them to recognize when they are running within an analysis environment.

Researchers must develop innovative methods to trick the malware into believing it is in a genuine system, enabling comprehensive analysis.

Additionally, real-world cases often uncover the involvement of nation-state actors or advanced persistent threats (APTs) targeting high-value assets.

These adversaries possess significant resources and employ highly sophisticated malware to achieve their goals.

Analysts scrutinize APT attacks to gain insights into their tactics, attribution, and potential motivations.

By understanding APTs, organizations can better defend against these formidable threats and implement appropriate security measures.

Furthermore, malware analysis reveals the exploitation of zero-day vulnerabilities, which are previously unknown and unpatched security flaws in software or hardware.

Advanced adversaries may use zero-day exploits to gain unauthorized access to systems.

Studying real-world cases of zero-day exploitation helps security professionals recognize the signs of such attacks and develop mitigation strategies.

Malware analysis also plays a critical role in threat intelligence, enabling the collection and dissemination of information about emerging threats.

Sharing insights from real-world cases with the broader cybersecurity community fosters collaboration and collective defense against malicious actors.

Threat intelligence feeds, reports, and indicators of compromise (IOCs) derived from malware analysis contribute to proactive threat detection and response.

In some cases, malware analysis reveals the use of ransomware, which encrypts victims' data and demands a ransom for its release.

Researchers examine ransomware variants to identify weaknesses in their encryption algorithms and develop decryption tools. By providing victims with decryption options, analysts can mitigate the impact of ransomware attacks.

Moreover, real-world cases of malware analysis often highlight the importance of incident response and coordination among security teams. Effective incident response involves identifying the scope of an attack, isolating affected systems, and containing the threat. Collaboration among IT, security, and legal teams is essential to ensure a swift and coordinated response to incidents.

Additionally, malware analysts collaborate with law enforcement agencies to track down and apprehend cybercriminals responsible for malicious activities.

By providing law enforcement with evidence and technical details, analysts contribute to the prosecution of cybercriminals and the disruption of criminal networks.

In summary, expert insights derived from real-world malware analysis cases are invaluable resources for the cybersecurity community.

These insights offer a deeper understanding of evolving threats, attack techniques, and adversary motivations.

By studying these cases, security professionals can enhance their ability to detect, respond to, and mitigate cyber threats effectively.

The lessons learned from real-world malware analysis cases contribute to the development of robust cybersecurity practices, threat intelligence sharing, and collaborative efforts to protect digital ecosystems from malicious actors.

Conclusion

In the ever-evolving landscape of cybersecurity, the field of malware reverse engineering stands as a bulwark against the relentless tide of digital threats. The book bundle "Malware Reverse Engineering: Cracking the Code" encompasses a comprehensive journey through the intricacies of this vital discipline, offering a range of expertise from the novice to the expert. Across four meticulously crafted volumes, we have explored the essential foundations, the mastery of skills, the comprehensive analysis, and the pinnacle of advanced techniques in the realm of malware reverse engineering.

"Malware Reverse Engineering Essentials: A Beginner's Guide," our opening volume, laid the groundwork for aspiring analysts. It provided a firm foothold for those just embarking on their journey into the intricate world of malicious software. Here, readers gained a fundamental understanding of malware, its anatomy, and the tools needed to dissect and understand its inner workings.

"Mastering Malware Reverse Engineering: From Novice to Expert," the second installment, was designed to be the bridge between foundational knowledge and advanced expertise. It guided readers through progressively complex challenges, imparting the skills necessary to analyze a wide range of malware specimens effectively. Novices transformed into capable analysts with a thirst for more profound insights.

"Malware Analysis and Reverse Engineering: A Comprehensive Journey," our third book, lived up to its name by providing a comprehensive exploration of the subject. It delved into the intricacies of both static and dynamic analysis techniques, equipping readers with a holistic approach to dissecting malware. This volume was a substantial step toward becoming a proficient malware analyst, offering a rich tapestry of knowledge.

Our final volume, "Advanced Techniques in Malware Reverse Engineering: Expert-Level Insights," brought readers to the summit of expertise. It unveiled the most intricate and elusive aspects of malware analysis, exposing the dark corners of code obfuscation, anti-analysis measures, and complex communication protocols. This book was tailored for those who aspired to be at the forefront of the field, gaining insights from real-world case studies and expert-level guidance.

As we reach the conclusion of this book bundle, it is crucial to recognize that the battle against malware is ongoing. The threat landscape continues to evolve, with adversaries deploying increasingly sophisticated tactics. However, armed with the knowledge and skills acquired through these four volumes, readers are well-equipped to face these challenges head-on. Whether you are a novice taking your first steps or an expert refining your techniques, "Malware Reverse Engineering: Cracking the Code" serves as a valuable resource in your mission to safeguard digital environments from the perils of malicious software.

In closing, we extend our gratitude to all readers, from the curious beginners to the seasoned experts, for embarking on this journey with us. Together, we strengthen the defenses against cyber threats, for the pursuit of knowledge is a powerful weapon in the realm of cybersecurity. May your expertise in malware reverse engineering continue to grow, and may your efforts contribute to a safer digital world.

www.ingramcontent.com/pod-product-compliance
Lightning Source LLC
Chambersburg PA
CBHW071235050326
40690CB00011B/2126